"What a pleasure to find a book dealing with the profundities under-lying eating and mealtimes, especially as they relate to life beyond obesity, anorexia, or calories! This is an unexpectedly important book, particularly for someone raising children."

Vincent J. Felitti, MD
co-Principal Investigator of the Adverse
Childhood Experiences Study (ACES)

"With his own authentic self-reflection, Charlie Slaughter helps par-ents understand how to use two of their key possessions—their pow-er and their past—to positively impact children during mealtimes. He shows that when infused with love, care, and connection, par-ents' power and past can be transformed into gifts they bring to the table in feeding their children."

Robert C. Whitaker, MD, MPH
Professor of Public Health and Pediatrics
Temple University

"This book is a gift for parents who have ever struggled with a child's feeding. Charlie has transcended the mealtime battles with an un-derstanding of how to improve your emotional connections with your child. As parents, we want our children to succeed in life and be happy. We also want them to be healthy and safe. Mealtime is the intersection of WHAT to feed and HOW to feed our children. Charlie has taken on the secrets of powerful parenting and provided practical tools for building life skills with each meal we share togeth-er. Charlie also provides strategies to help heal our own relationship with food and give the gift of love and emotional connectedness with our children. In this book Charlie shines the light on putting the JOY back into enJOYment of eating. It is a gift for parents and an investment for healthy future generations."

Cheryl Alto, MS, RD
Nutrition Consultant, Oregon WIC Program

Hungry *for* *Love:*

Creating a mealtime environment that builds connection, life skills, and eating capabilities

Charlie Slaughter, MPH, RD

ISBN: 1480008583
ISBN 13: 9781480008588
Library of Congress Control Number: 2013923221
LCCN Imprint Name: CreateSpace Independent Publishing Platform
North Charleston, South Carolina

Table of Contents

Acknowledgments and Thanks

My Dad - thank you for your incredible love, support, on-going super-crazy delight in me, encouragement, belief in me, deep acceptance, patience, and belief in the need for my message to be heard and received by parents.

Betsy – for your deep and everlasting love and reminding me of the need to share what I had to say. Thank you for creating a safe, secure, nurturing, and truth-filled home and relationship. That secure base and safe haven allowed me to grow and be able to write this book. I love the incredibly rich and ever deeper life I have with you. Without you my life would have been a fraction of what it is.

Alika Hope – for your wonderful creativity, deep love, vision, and entrepreneurial spirit. You have made this book so much better, but, more importantly, you make the world a better place.

Melissa Vu from Vu Works - www.vu-works.com – for the wonderful front cover and art work. You nailed it with Air Force One.

Phyllis Meredith – http://phyllismeredith.com - for the wonderful photographs and for being the consummate professional.

Kent Hoffman – for being a deep friend and for the powerful way you live. I'm awed at the number of lives you have deeply touched and all of the additional love and joy in this world you have helped to release.

Cheryl Alto – for your long-term support and encouragement to get this message out to parents and providers and for your commitment to strengthening parent-child relationships. I thank you for your long-term friendship. That has been a gift.

Vincent Felitti – for seeing value in my writing and my message and helping me to be published.

Bob Whitaker –thank you for the many times you supported me and for the opportunities to expand and deepen my thinking. I love your integrity and deep commitment.

Monica Belyea – for your support and sound advice to not make the book too long or too complicated.

Muriel Hastings – for sharing your story of standing up for your daughter. Our world needs more people like you.

David Hovey – you helped me turn my fears into strengths, helped me to use my power, and helped me to find, own, and honor my voice. This book would not have happened without you.

Eleni Despotopoulos – my beloved granddaughter who gives me such deep joy and brings me more life. I love your zest for life.

George Despotopoulos – my beloved grandson who gives me such deep joy and brings me more life. I love all of the adventures we take.

Don – many, many thanks for listening, listening, and listening to me and for your on-going encouragement and friendship. You are a gem.

My many colleagues and attachment champions – thank you for sharing life with me and for sharing so generously. You've made my life so much richer and enjoyable.

Ronald Rolheiser – for sharing your amazing wisdom and deep, life-giving perspective in <u>Against an Infinite Horizon</u>. I love the way you provide the bigger picture and help life make sense. You have provided me with immense comfort and restored me to peace in my early morning bouts of anxiety. You helped deepen my sense of the potential for releasing more love and giving more life through our relationships. You are such a blessing.

Susan Ashton – for your wonderful writing, deep truth, and performance in "You Move Me." What a gift.

Welcome

There are two huge challenges in our country. One challenge is that many of our young children and kids are experiencing a deficit of genuine love. As a result, they are growing up less capable, less curious, less passionate, less secure, and less influential. Their healthy development is being compromised.

The other problem is that many parents are missing opportunities to provide the kind of parenting that is actually powerful in its impact on their children's healthy development. As a result, many parents are missing opportunities of having the joy and inner satisfaction of providing powerful parenting that helps their kids thrive in life.

Mealtimes are one of the best places to provide the genuine love young children and kids need. Mealtimes are also an opportunity-rich place for a parent to provide the strong type of parenting that is so satisfying to parents.

Mealtimes can either build emotional connection, or they can build emotional disconnection between a child and their parent. Mealtimes can either build a deep sense of trust, or they can build distrust and despair in a child. Mealtimes can build a genuine joy of exploring or build a desire to self-protect rather than explore.

Mealtimes can build a child's enjoyment and even joy about eating or build anxiety, ambivalence, and even displeasure about eating. Mealtimes can be a time of enjoyment and relaxation for parents or a time of stress and dread.

Mealtimes can help build important life skills and healthy eating capabilities or result in limitations to a child's eating capabilities and life skills.

The bad news is that these unhealthy traits, capabilities, and life skills will be carried by kids into their adult years. These unhealthy traits, capabilities, and life skills will limit their success in life and fullness of life.

A child who learns from experience that she is loved, cared for, welcomed, accepted, safe, and delighted in is given a great foundation for thriving and enjoying life. A healthy mealtime environment will help provide these experiences for your child.

The good news is that a parent can adopt strategies that build healthy mealtime environments at any time and still have an impact on their kids' healthy development. It is never too late. Additionally, adoption of strategies that build healthy mealtime environments will also have an impact on the mealtime strategies used by your kids when they grow up and become parents.

This book provides you with skills, strategies, concepts, and insights to help you develop a developmentally healthy mealtime environment for your family. As a result, you will be able to create and sustain a mealtime environment that builds emotional connection, trust, enjoyment, life skills, and eating capabilities. Additionally, these mealtime environment changes will help make parenting more satisfying and family meals less stressful for you.

My goal is to help and support you in achieving an important goal - being a good enough parent. Not a perfect parent, but a good enough parent.

I've been profoundly influenced by a new parenting intervention that is quite unique – Circle of Security Parenting© (COS P).[1] Part of its uniqueness is its focus on building parents' basic relationship capabilities. When a parent has the basic relationship capabilities, the parent now has the basic tools and skills to provide a pattern of caregiving that builds secure attachment. This in turn results in kids being much more likely to thrive in life. It also results in big improvements in children's behavior. I'll explain some more about COS P in a later chapter and also share about some of the COS P concepts in various parts of the book. COS P is simply the best love and joy building and life-giving intervention I've ever encountered

One of the most powerful things I've learned from COS P and studying the research on attachment, is that the quality of the parent-child relationship creates the foundation for kids' future development. Kids with a secure attachment have a strong, secure foundation while kids with an insecure or disorganized attachment have a weakened or even quite damaged foundation. In turn, a child's foundation supports, hinders, or dramatically interferes with their future development. I view COS P as now giving communities, for the first time ever, a tool to help many more kids have or shift toward a secure attachment. In turn, I think this has profound implications for kids' learning, quality of future relationships, employment, and the quality of life in communities.

Reflection is a key process for a parent to become more loving and more powerful. Reflection allows you to reflect on your child's behavior and allows you to reflect on your reaction to your child's behavior. Reflection also allows you to reflect on the parenting you received and to reflect on how that shaped who you are today. I've included a "Food for Thought" section after the beginning of the book and after each chapter that includes some questions to help spark some reflection about what you've just read and about your mealtime experiences with your child. Additionally, the questions can allow some reflection about your own childhood mealtime experiences. If you belong to a book club, these questions can help move the conversations into some intimate sharing and honest dialogue.

My one hope is that this book will help you provide more genuine love in your family, help your child be able to receive more of your love, and help your child grow in their life skills and eating capabilities.

A Word to Parents

I have been a parent for 37 years and a specialist in the field of nutrition and early childhood development for 38 years. One important value I realized years ago I have is a genuine desire to see parents and children thrive in life. When I see someone thriving in life, that gives me joy.

I've tried to write this book in a way that parents have a sense of me being on their side. If my writing helps you or your child to thrive in life, that is, in my eyes, a success.

As a parent and as someone who has worked with parents, I know parenting is hard work; it can be challenging work, and it can be frustrating work. Parenting also gives many opportunities to be generous by helping our children grow into capable, loving adults.

My focus is not on perfect parenting; it is on good enough parenting.

I believe that good enough parenting is a huge gift to your child. I also believe that good enough parenting is a huge gift to our nation and to the world. Good enough parenting creates more trust, care, and genuine love in families, our communities, our nation and the world. We need more genuine love, care, and trust in all of these places.

Some of what you read may bring you a challenge about parenting or about your own life. You may realize you are being called to stop certain parenting behaviors and try some new parenting behaviors. This type of change is difficult but is possible.

As you read through this book and think about your parenting and the parenting you received, I hope you can take in the words and thoughts of this book and hear them as coming from someone on your side. Please remember I did not write this book to be judgmental toward you or any other parent. I have tried to write to reflect my own approach of accepting each parent as they are today and then coming alongside them as someone who is genuinely interested in their well-being and as someone on their side.

Much of my work with parents has exposed me to the fact that many people working with parents come across as being critical of their parenting, which is not helpful at all since it causes shame, builds distrust, and doesn't give the parent a sense of the person being on their side.

While my primary focus has been to write in a way that helps build everyday parenting that is powerful and in a way that genuinely attracts parents to making changes about their mealtimes, I also know that my writing may bring a new awareness to you about your parenting or even about the parenting you received.

Your new awareness can result in a new challenge in your life. I am convinced that each of us is called to grow throughout our life so that we have more and more genuine love, care, and trust. My experience is that it is a challenge that leads to a positive change and growth. If there are no challenges, then there is little growth.

So, I hope any challenges this book brings into your life will be seen as a gift of genuine love.

The 30 Second Book
(and a little more)

If you leave with nothing else, I want you to leave with this perspective:

> **Four things are fed by you at a meal:**
> **1. Love**
> **2. Care**
> **3. Connection**
> **4. Food**

The food is important, but your love, your care, and your connection are far more important than the food.

<u>This is very important for you and for your child. So let me say it again.</u>

The food is important, but your love, your care, and your connection are far more important than the food.

My Perspective

When a parent offers these four things: love, care, connection, and food, you provide powerful parenting. Your child thrives, and you thrive. Parenting becomes easier and more satisfying. Your child receives better support for his healthy development. You and your child end up with a more positive and emotionally connected relationship. That is both powerful and priceless.

The rest of the book is about how you can make this transformation happen and why your presence at meals, your interactions at meals, your expectations, and the mealtime environment you create are so powerful. The outcome is your child wins, and you win. That is wonderful and life-giving parenting.

Two things to keep in mind:

1. If your child comes to a meal with little or no appetite at a meal, the mealtime is still a great opportunity to offer your child your love, care, and connection. Your child is still hungry for these life-giving gifts from you.

2. Your child is **<u>always</u>** more important than the food.

Parental Love

At its simplest this book is about providing genuine love. As you read this book, keep in mind that parental love has two components: Nurture and Structure[2]. Nurture is about offering your genuine interest, care, warmth, and support. Nurture is also about delighting in your child and offering your genuine acceptance. Structure is about providing developmentally appropriate limits and challenges so your child is able to grow to be a more capable and a more loving person. Healthy nurture and healthy structure are each an act of genuine love. Each is equally important.

Enjoy.

Food for Thought

1. What was your response to the statement that three other things are fed at a meal besides the food?

2. How did you respond to the statement that your love, care, and connection are more important to your child than the food?

3. What's one thing about your child's eating you like? What is one thing about your child's eating that frustrates or concerns you?

4. What kind of mealtime environment would you like to create for your family? Is this similar to or different from the mealtime environment you had in your own childhood?

CHAPTER 1:

Some Thoughts on Genuine Love and on Power

I use the phrase "genuine love" throughout the book. At its simplest, genuine love is love that builds and supports an emotional connection with your child while also taking action that builds your child's life skills and capacity to thrive in life. Genuine love understands the importance of appropriate challenges to a child's growth while also providing loving support during the challenges.

It is important to look at the components of genuine love. Not only is genuine love composed of nurture and structure, it also has a specific intent, is freely given, is developmentally supportive, and builds trust. Additionally, for your love to have an impact, it requires your presence and your power.

Nurture and Structure

Genuine love has two parts - nurture and structure. Nurture can be a warm and soothing touch or an accepting or delighted look. It is saying "I love you" and meaning it. It is a warm hug, a reassuring pat on the back, or a reassuring word.

Structure, on the other hand, can be setting appropriate limits or boundaries that help a child feel safe yet still allow healthy development. Structure can be providing a small challenge by offering a new food yet being present in a supportive way.

Both nurture and structure require your presence at the meal. If you are not present with your child, you cannot be there to provide your nurture or your structure. Quite simply, your presence is foundational.

Nurture will let a child know he has worth. Structure will let a child know he has worth. Yet, the way for a child to develop the strongest internal belief he has worth is to receive both nurture and structure.

Specific Intent

Genuine love has a specific intent of seeing the person thrive in a healthy way. It is not love given to control the person or love given with an expectation that love will be returned to you at the same time. When I offer my genuine love, I delight that my child receives it. But, if my child cannot receive it, I don't get angry at my child or withdraw emotionally from my child.

Freely Given

Genuine love is actually given freely because you can't help but give it away. Basically, you have genuine love in you because, most likely, you have first received genuine love. I think each parent, including myself, has parts of ourselves where we don't have genuine love. If I haven't received it myself, then it is next to impossible to give something I don't have. It doesn't make me a bad person; I just don't have it to give.

The other possible cause is that I was wounded in this area by my parents' lack of caring (neglect) or meanness to me. Quite likely, our parents may have been wounded in this same area and could not give us the genuine love we needed. My understanding from my own struggles and healing with my own woundedness is that my woundedness creates a barrier to either receiving or offering genuine love. In essence the work then becomes about addressing each barrier to receiving and giving genuine love. Frankly, when you spend time with an infant, toddler, preschooler, child, or adolescent, you will have numerous opportunities to become aware of your own barriers to receiving or giving love.

Of course, the next question then becomes, "Do I want to grow in being able to give genuine love in this area of my life?" This kind of growth work is hard but quite rewarding. Each gift I have received from going through the hard work of addressing the barrier has always been better than what I had to surrender. Ultimately, it allows me to love in a healthy way without giving myself up.

Developmentally Supportive

Genuine love is also developmentally supportive. For example, the physical affection you give your newborn by holding him in your arms and making joyful baby sounds to him is absolutely developmentally appropriate. If you were to do the same behavior with your 17 year old son, it would be developmentally inappropriate. Thus, this behavior would be developmentally supportive with the newborn but not developmentally supportive to your 17 year old.

Preschools that allow and expect preschoolers to pour milk from a small pitcher into their cup are being developmentally supportive because they know kids that age are capable of learning to pour milk from a small pitcher. They also know that having spills is part of the learning process. They will then help the child learn to clean up their spill but do so in a supportive way so the child has the experience of someone stronger, kind, and wise being on their side. They know it is important to support learning to pour from a pitcher. They also know it is important for a child to receive a natural consequence by having to clean up the spill. Additionally, they know it is very important not to humiliate, blame, or shame the child for making a spill, but, rather, to treat it in a matter of fact and low-key way.

A parent offering a new food to a child is being developmentally supportive. Staying neutral about your child's response each time to trying the new food is being developmentally supportive.

Trusting that your child knows how much or how little he needs to eat at any meal is developmentally supportive. Trusting that your child will actually eat as much or as little as he needs in order to be

3

satisfied is developmentally supportive. Trusting that if you provide a healthy mealtime environment your child will learn, at his own pace, to like a variety of foods is developmentally supportive.

Trusting that your love, care, and connection are more important than how much your child eats at a meal is developmentally support- ive. Trusting that sometimes your struggle about your child's eating may be an indication that you have an issue that needs to be ad- dressed, and your child doesn't, is developmentally supportive.

Making your child eat all of his food, even if he isn't hungry, is not being developmentally supportive. Neither is pressuring or requir- ing him to eat a food he doesn't like. However, going to the opposite extreme and not offering new foods to your child is not developmen- tally supportive either because part of being developmentally sup- portive is offering an appropriate challenge to a child.

Using mealtime to share your anger about your child's behavior is not developmentally supportive. Having your child keep quiet during the entire mealtime is not developmentally supportive. Having mealtimes always be a serious and somber time is not developmentally supportive.

What this book tries to accomplish is to help you find the develop- mentally healthy middle ground. You do this by creating and staying in a developmentally supportive mealtime environment while still en- suring your child receives developmentally appropriate challenges.

Trust Building
Having genuine trust in others and about the world is a wonder- ful gift for an infant, child, adolescent, and even an adult to have. Helping a child develop their own internal and genuine sense of trust begins with and depends on the parent.

Basically, you want your child to have a pattern of mealtime experi- ences that results in the following internal beliefs being created in your child. An internal belief is something the child knows in his heart because the internal belief has been created from a consistent set of experiences that happen over and over so there has been a pattern created. An internal belief is not based on what has been said to the child; it is based on what the child has experienced and the pattern of those experiences. For example, if there is enough food at each meal, your child has a pattern of experience that there is always enough food. His experience teaches him that there is always enough food. He grows to expect and to trust that there will be enough food at each meal.

I think there are nine core beliefs about trust you want your child to receive from the mealtime environment you create:

1. I can trust there will be enough food.

2. I can trust an adult will be at the table with me and will offer their love, care, and connection.

3. I can trust that mealtimes will be pleasant.

4. I can trust that mealtimes will be a time of safety and emotional connection.

5. If there is a rupture in our relationship, I can trust a wise and caring adult will take the necessary steps to repair the rupture and restore our relationship.

6. I can trust that I will be able to be in charge of how much I eat, even if I choose to eat very little, eat none at all, or ask for additional helpings.

7. I can trust I will routinely encounter foods I have never or rarely seen before.

8. I can trust I will be supported in a way that helps me learn to like most new foods.

9. I can trust when I encounter a challenge about a new food or expectation about my behavior, a caring adult will help me successfully deal with the challenge and allow me to deal with it at my own pace.

An integral part of building trust at meals is using mealtime strategies that are developmentally supportive. Strategies that are developmentally supportive will have a foundation of giving your child the experience of having a parent on his side. But, it doesn't end there. Developmentally supportive parenting will include a parental expectation that their child can grow in capability with his eating and his mealtime behavior. As a result, developmentally supportive parenting will also provide developmentally appropriate challenges to give your child achievable opportunities to grow in his eating and mealtime capabilities.

A Simple Way to View Your Child's Behavior

The Circle of Security Parenting© (COS P) developers created a simple, easy-to-understand, non-shaming, and quite useful approach to understanding children's behavior. Here is one of the drawings they use.[3]

The parent provides the two hands on the Circle. When a child has the top hand, the secure base, the child has an internal sense of emotional safety and inner security. Having this internal sense of emotional safety and inner security allows the child's innate desire for exploring to kick in, and the child goes out to explore. Of course, exploration for an infant, a toddler, an elementary age child, or an adolescent will each look different, but it is still exploration. Your child still needs something from you while exploring, and COS P has a simple way for you to figure out what your child needs from you. Your child needs you to watch over him, enjoy with him, delight in him, or help him.

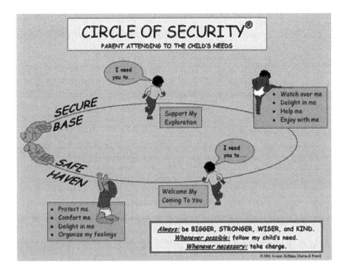

Inevitably, a child will experience distress while exploring. The child may feel discomfort, become tired, become frightened, or may just need to reconnect with you at an emotional level. The child needs the bottom hand to welcome him back in for comfort, protection, delight, or help with organizing his feelings.

The beauty of this drawing and approach is parents can say to themselves, "Is my child at the top of the Circle exploring **or** is my child at the bottom of the Circle needing to be welcomed in?" Parents love the simplicity, usefulness, and beauty of this relationship tool. Basically, the Circle is what genuine love looks like.

I am finding from my work to bring COS P to communities that many mothers and fathers, regardless of education level or level of income, love what COS P teaches them and love how COS P improves their relationship with their children. We're also hearing that it helps parents better understand why each other acts the way they do. Even better, we're seeing good parents become more powerful parents by becoming stronger at the top of the Circle or stronger at the bottom of the Circle. If you struggle with building a stronger connection with your child or struggle with under-using or over-using your power, COS P can help you make the shift to using your power with love.

If you ever have an opportunity to take part in a Circle of Security Parenting© group, I highly encourage you to do so. Your life and your children's lives will be much richer.

If you find yourself having struggles about how you react to your child's behavior and can't seem to get out of your pattern of reaction, COS P can be very valuable in giving you the tools and insights to get out of your pattern of reaction. You can find out if someone in your area is offering COS P by going to www.circleofsecurity.net and then clicking on the Parents tab.

Power and Love

As you read through this book, you will find a consistent and primary focus on love, particularly a parent's love. I happen to believe a parent's love is a very powerful force. I also know that many parents are blocked in being able to offer their love in certain aspects of parenting due to some very powerful reasons. I also believe many parents have room to grow and learn how they do and do not offer love. I don't believe any one parent has it all together. Each of us is called to increase our capability to genuinely offer love and to reduce our unhealthy ways of offering love.

There is also a consistent theme and focus on power in this book. Parental power is about taking charge when that is necessary and appropriate but also providing a pattern of opportunities for their child to be in charge when that is appropriate. Use of power is healthy when it has this purpose and is used to support and build a child's healthy development.

I believe every parent has power, and every parent uses their power. However, we live in an age that avoids the issue of power and avoids the issue of power and love. Yet, I find many parents are hungry to dialogue about their use of power and dialogue about their child having and using power. At a gut level, I find many parents get it that they need to have one foot in the arena of using their power while at the same time have the other foot in the arena of helping their child to have and use power. The healthy goal for the parent is to find the balance of the parent having and using their power **and** helping their child have and use power so their child's capability and capacity for love and competency grows.

I understand a parent may use their power to build their child's capability and to help their child thrive in life. I also understand, because of a parent's woundedness in how power was used against them in their own childhood, a parent may be unwilling to use their power in certain or in many areas of their life, including areas of parenting. Additionally, because of their own woundedness, a parent may have some deep struggles with letting their child have and use power.

A key aspect to a parent using their power is agenda setting. That is, what agenda are you consciously setting for your child's development? My focus is helping parents set a developmentally healthy agenda for their mealtime environment. Some parents have already done this. Some parents want to do this but don't yet have the tools and strategies to do so. Some parents have set an agenda of wanting their children to be happy. A happy child is a good agenda. However, I think a more powerful agenda is a child who is growing in capability and love, that is, love of self, love of others, and love of learning.

If you can state what your family's mealtime agenda is, that is great. If not, you could start with a simple agenda and grow your agenda at a pace that works for you. For example, you might say your agenda will be to sit and share a meal, such as dinner, with your kids four times a week. Or you may decide your initial agenda is to not allow the TV or any electronic toys or phones to be turned on during the meal. The key piece here is to have an agenda that works for you and is supportive of your child's healthy development. I think this book can be an ally to you in developing a strong and developmentally savvy agenda. Having an agenda that is developmentally healthy is a huge gift to your child. It is also an act of love to yourself and to your child. Additionally, it is a gift you contribute to the quality of your community.

9

A key focus of this book is helping parents learn about and acquire some basic tools and concepts that help parents use their power and love to build a developmentally healthy mealtime environment.

The most important task is to use both your love and your power, but in a way that involves an active seeking of balance between these two forces. I say active seeking of balance because a child's developmental stage and needs will change. There may be instances where you need to focus more on love and instances where you may need to focus more on power. But every child, no matter their age, still needs your love and your power.

Patterns of Power and Love

One out-of-balance pattern is to use your power but not your love. This builds emotional disconnection and aloneness rather than the joy of emotional connection. You may achieve compliance but you aren't building resilient capability. You also don't help your child acquire through experience the genuine and treasured joy of exploring and learning. This pattern also builds distrust and can build internalized fear in your child.

A second out-of-balance pattern is to use your love but not your power. With this pattern, your child misses out on receiving challenges that help build your child's internal sense of being capable and learning to deal with a challenge until finally resolving the challenge.

A third out-of-balance pattern is to neither use your love nor use your power. This is a pretty tough situation for a child.

A fourth and developmentally healthy pattern is for a parent to use both their power and their love. A parent who uses both of these will also want their child to have experiences of having power and using their power. This parent understands their child needs to have many opportunities to have and use power. This parent knows this will build their child's capability. This parent also realizes if their child has a pattern of caregiving in which their child also receives love while using and after using power, this becomes a powerful way of parenting. This book will give many examples of parents using both their power and their love.

Kids and Power

The trick for a parent in helping their child have and use power is to do it in a way that the child gains power over the years, but not at the expense of the parent losing power. That is, don't do this in a way that the child gains power because the parent gives up their power to their child. Instead, help your child acquire experiences of having and using power in the areas where it is appropriate for the child to be using power. For example, a parent, and not the two-year-old child, will choose what foods to have at dinner. Yet, a parent of a 16 year-old teenager who has been working over the years to involve their child in food selection and meal preparation could easily let their teenager be in charge of selecting what foods the teenager will prepare for dinner several nights a week.

Kids need to be able to practice having and using power. This provides them with some very valuable experience. They learn it is normal to have and use power. They learn about the joy of accomplishment and the natural consequences that occur from using their power. They learn how their use of power can build connection or can build disconnection. Just as importantly, kids also need an environment that provides and supports these experiences. Kids need parents who use their power but use it in a loving way and use it in a developmentally savvy way. The focus for a parent is not on using power to control, although that is necessary at times. The focus is using your power to grow and support your child's capability and grow your child's sense of being genuinely loved.

As you read this book, there are a number of examples of parents using their power and doing so in a developmentally healthy way. You will also encounter a number of examples of kids having and using power during mealtimes.

A parent who has a pattern of parenting with love and power will have a multi-prong agenda of building connection and building capability. A parent with this agenda will be comfortable offering their love **and** using their power. That makes it much easier to provide and allow developmentally appropriate challenges for their child. They know challenges are how a child best learns to become more capable in life. However, they know in their hearts that providing or allowing a challenge needs to include emotional connection and just enough support during and after the challenge so their child can grow in capability. That is also why these parents will have appropriate expectations for their child's behavior at mealtimes. They know their expectations will provide a challenge to their child. However, they are savvy enough to know the expectation needs to be appropriate for their child's developmental stage so it isn't too big of a challenge. As you read this book, you will get a sense of the ways this can be done at mealtimes.

Food for Thought

1. Discuss what it means to be developmentally supportive. Who has been developmentally supportive in your life?

2. Of the nine core beliefs about trust, which two are the most important for your child to receive?

3. What caught your attention about parents having and using power?

4. What caught your attention about parents helping their kids have and use power?

CHAPTER 2:

A Perspective on Struggles with Your Child's Eating

Being 57 years of age as I write this chapter, I can now say all of the healing that has resulted in me being able to receive more love, give more love, trust more, and have more confidence would not have happened without first having a struggle. No struggle, no growth.

The other essential truth is that nearly all of my struggles have taken place because of a relationship with someone – my spouse, my mom, my dad, my friends, my bosses, my kids, my co-workers, my neighbors, …

Usually, my first reaction to a new struggle is to get angry at the person, attack them, blame them, expect them to change, pull back from them physically or emotionally, or deny there is a problem.

None of these reactions leads to growth. What I now realize is these reactions were strategies I used as attempts to protect myself. But all they did was "protect" me from gaining awareness of some uncomfortable truths I preferred to avoid.

In a similar way, the struggles you have with your child's eating or mealtime behavior can be because of any of the following reasons:

- Not having strategies that build your child's eating capabilities.

- Not having strategies that allow you to provide a mealtime environment that builds genuine emotional connection with your child.

- Not having an understanding of the different factors that help and hinder your child learning to like a new food.

- Holding on to the belief that whether your child eats a particular food or eats all her food is more important to you than your child's connection with you.

- Being at the table with your child during a meal is painful to you or makes you very uncomfortable because of your own childhood experiences.

I'll go into all of these reasons later on, but let's start with a brief look at the last one, because your experience there can affect the ways you approach the others on the list.

Your struggle with your child's mealtime behavior can be connected with your own eating experiences and patterns of experiences when you were a child. Perhaps, as a child, you were not treated as if you were capable of growing in your eating capability. Maybe you were forced to clean your plate or forced to eat a food you didn't like. Perhaps no adult sat at the table with you when you ate. Maybe there wasn't enough food to satisfy your hunger. Maybe your parents seemed more interested in their drugs or alcohol than in providing food on a regular basis or providing enough food on a regular basis. Maybe mealtime was tense or unpleasant; that could affect your feelings and beliefs about family meals and the mealtime environment. Maybe there was tension because you didn't know if your parent or another adult at the table was going to blow up or what would set them off. Maybe there was physical, sexual, and/or emotional abuse going on in your home, or maybe you were experiencing emotional or physical neglect in your home. After all, no meal would be enjoyable under those circumstances.

Maybe you've tried to tuck away those old memories or perhaps you decided you would do the opposite with your kids and never treat them the way you were treated. But the old stuff is still there. And it is still influencing your interactions with your child

One book, <u>Giving the Love that Heals</u>, by Harville Hendrix and Helen Hunt, shares how a parent often struggles when their own child reaches an age or developmental stage that is the same when the parent had bad experiences at this same age or developmental stage.[4] For example, when you were about 18 months old and said "No. I don't want to eat that" at the family meal, you may have been punished, shamed, and/or rejected. When your own child reaches 18 months and starts to say "No." you may have a reaction that seems to come out of nowhere. You may find yourself automatically treating your 18 month old child the same way you had been treated, even though you had no intention of treating your child that way.

Basically, your old wound is driving your behavior. An old wound has a very strong emotional component to it. Your emotional reaction is quite strong and quite quick, which is good because it helps grab your attention. In fact, your emotional response will be stronger than your thinking and stronger than your intent to parent well.

All of this is just to say you need to be kind and loving to yourself as you start to look closer at your struggles, frustrations, and concerns about your child's eating. Certainly there is understanding you can gain and strategies you can learn that will help. But your struggles can also be a doorway to stopping, taking the focus off your child, focusing on yourself, and looking deeper to see if your difficulties are also connected with your own experience as a child.

Again, I have found Circle of Security Parenting© (COS P) to be extremely helpful to parents in gaining awareness of their lightening quick, over-the-top, negative reactions to a behavior of their infant, child, or teenager. COS P has several simple but powerful tools that help break this action-reaction cycle. For example, some of the first parents in Spokane, Washington who received the original Circle of Security intervention came up with a term – Shark Music – to name this type of reaction in themselves. I'll discuss this more in a later chapter.

Food for Thought

1. How might your child's eating struggles be connected to your own childhood eating struggles?

2. This chapter mentions the need to be kind and loving to yourself as you start looking at your mealtime struggles with your child. List three ways to be kind and loving to yourself.

CHAPTER 3:

Some Basic Strategies for Building a Safe, Nurturing, and Developmentally Challenging Mealtime Environment

My colleague, Mavis Bomengen, a public health nurse in Lakeview, Oregon, shared a story with me about a mom whose toddler would not stay in the high chair when she was being fed. As Mavis talked with the mom, she learned that the toddler was given a bottle whenever the toddler asked for it. Mavis recommended the toddler only be fed approximately every 2 ½ -3 hours and not in between. The mom agreed to go home and try this new strategy. A week later Mavis received a call from the mom who said, "Mavis, you won't believe it. She is now begging to get into the high chair."

The way Mavis worked with this mom in a respectful way and offered a helpful strategy is important. But more importantly, this mom chose, out of her love for her child, to use her power to set a developmentally healthy schedule of when her toddler would be given opportunities to eat. By adopting the schedule for her toddler of offering food approximately every 2 ½ -3 hours and not in between, the mom also provided a developmentally healthy schedule that helped her toddler come to the high chair with a good appetite.

This book will cover a number of eating capabilities and life skills that a parent can build in their child at mealtimes. At its heart though, these eating capabilities and life skills are built by developing a healthy mealtime environment that uses a few basic strategies, including the strategy used by the mom in the story above.

However, before we go any further, let's look at the three basic strategies.

1. Using Your Power Wisely and with Love

Kids need parents who use their power. But, even more importantly, kids need parents who use their power wisely **and** with love.

There are parts of mealtimes where the parent, and not the child, needs to be using their power. One goal for the parent is to use to use their power to build a developmentally healthy mealtime environment.

For example, in order to build connection at mealtime, the parent will use their power to have their child join the meal so everyone is at the same place at the same time. This alone doesn't build connection, but, if a parent doesn't use their power to do this, there will be no opportunity to build connection at a mealtime. A parent will use their power to keep the mealtime environment emotionally safe and pleasant. A parent will use their power to encourage and support conversations and inclusion of everyone in the conversations.

Parents also use their power to decide what foods will be offered at a meal or snack. A parent's job is to be in charge of what food is purchased, prepared, and provided. This is not your child's job. When your child is old enough, you can start to involve your child in this, but the responsibility is still with the parent. Children are neither knowledgeable nor wise enough to be making the decision about what foods will be provided at meals and at snacks.

A developmentally savvy parent will wisely use their power to build a mealtime environment that not only allows their child to experience genuine emotional connection but also helps their child acquire important life skills and eating capabilities.

Another vital and often overlooked aspect of mealtimes is the opportunity for parents to provide on-going opportunities for their child to have and use power. Children need on-going practice with having and using power, and, even more importantly, receiving permission and support to have and use power. Children need this to be able to grow into adults who are comfortable having and using power.

When you allow your child to have power about how much he eats and the power to decide whether or not to eat a food at a meal or snack, you are giving your child a wonderful opportunity to have and use his power. This also makes parenting easier since the parent no longer has to take on the job of being in charge of the amount of food their child eats or whether their child eats a particular food at a meal or snack.

Later chapters in the book explore in greater detail this concept of parents having and using their power and allowing their child to have and use some power. I'll also go into more detail about the life skills and eating capabilities built by parents using their power and allowing their child to have and use some power.

2. Being Developmentally Savvy

There is a force at work in your child that you can ignore or fight as you parent your child, or you can tap into it and make parenting easier. Basically, each child is created with an internal drive to develop and grow. In a sense, each child is created to have an internal drive or desire to grow in capability. I remember walking into my oldest daughter's room when she was 3 or 4 years old and finding that she had attached a shoe lace to a handle on her dresser. It turns out she took the initiative to spend time on her own learning to tie a bow knot. That revealed to me her internal drive to grow in capability.

When you provide a developmentally healthy mealtime environment you provide an environment that allows your child's developmental forces to be at work, and you help him grow to be more competent.

Additionally, each child is unique. A child's uniqueness will show up at mealtimes. Your child may not like foods to touch, may want to mix all of them together, or may not be concerned at all if they touch or are mixed together. Your child may be quicker to learn to like new foods or may go at a much slower pace. One mom recently shared with me that her son took five years before he learned to like broccoli. She kept serving it because she liked it, never pressured her child to eat it, and never turned it into a battle. If he never ever ate broccoli, that would have been acceptable to her too.

However, don't automatically assume a child's initial negative reaction to a food is a sign of your child's uniqueness. It may be, but it is more likely the child is going through the normal reactions to a new food. Remember, most kids can learn to like most foods when given a mealtime environment that allows them to learn to like a new food at their own pace while providing developmentally appropriate support and challenges.

A third way to be developmentally savvy is to build a mealtime environment that helps your child come to the meal or snack with a good appetite. Kids who come to a meal with a good appetite are better eaters and are more likely to try a new food.

A fourth way of being developmentally savvy is to build a mealtime environment that provides opportunities for your child to explore and to provide reassurance and support as he encounters struggles as he explores.

A fifth way of being developmentally savvy is to build a mealtime environment that provides positive emotional connection. This starts with you sitting and being with your child at each meal and snack. If you don't, your child will miss an important opportunity to receive more of your love, care, and connection. You make the difference between mealtime being a time of emotional disconnection or a time of emotional connection; a time of feeling overwhelmed and unsupported or a time of learning to deal with a small challenge and having the loving support of a parent; an unpleasant and tense time or a time of enjoyment and relaxation.

If you'd like to learn more about developmental stages and children's eating, I recommend Ellyn Satter's book, <u>Child of Mine</u>. It describes each developmental stage and how the child's developmental needs and drives play out during feeding and mealtimes from early infancy through childhood and into adolescence.

3. Offering Developmentally Appropriate Challenges

Part of a parent's job is allowing or even providing your child an opportunity to have a developmentally appropriate challenge. Challenges are developmentally important because they provide your child an opportunity to gain a sense of accomplishment and to grow in capability. Those are great gifts.

I keep talking about a developmentally appropriate challenge. A developmentally <u>inappropriate</u> challenge is one that is beyond a child's capacity. Asking a three-year old to pour milk from a small pitcher into their cup while sitting at a table is a developmentally appropriate challenge. Asking a six-month old infant to do the same thing would be a developmentally <u>inappropriate</u> challenge.

That is also why your child needs you to be present at the table. Your child needs your support and reassurance to help him learn to deal with a developmentally appropriate challenge. Your presence and support are crucial and important gifts to your child as he faces and then deals successfully with a challenge.

Your Mealtime Environment Goal

As I've spoken with parents, preschool teachers and staff, and health professionals about mealtime environments, I've come to understand that mealtime environments fall into three patterns. At one extreme is the unstructured mealtime environment. At the other extreme is the rigid mealtime environment. What I work with people to build is what I call a safe, nurturing, and developmentally challenging mealtime environment.

Many parents have not been exposed to a developmentally healthy mealtime environment. This developmentally healthy middle ground has some aspects of the other two environments but has more sanity, emotional connection, and more support for kids' healthy development. Based on feedback from parents, I find this developmentally healthy middle ground makes parenting easier and more satisfying.

Before I talk about each of the three mealtime environments, I want to say a few things about what I'm not saying. I think parenting is quite challenging, and no parent does it perfectly. It is also easy to criticize a parent. My hope is that I come across as being on your side and not critical of you. I also hope to show you some possibilities about life being better for you and for your child.

My job is not to tell you to change or force you to change. My hope is to connect with and support your own genuine, internal desire to change. I have attempted to write this book in a way that does not condemn or judge you. If I have failed, please accept my apology because that has not been my intent, and I hope you will forgive me.

Unstructured Mealtime Environment

© Phyllis Meredith – www.phyllismeredith.com

At one extreme, a mealtime environment can be lacking parental power. Kids can eat when they want, where they want, and what they want. In an unstructured mealtime, the parent is not using their power to set when and where their child will eat and for choosing what foods will be offered to their child. Family members are eating at different times, eating at different places in the home, and/or eating different foods. If you saw a videotape of this kind of mealtime environment, you might see a child going into the kitchen at anytime of the day and getting the food he wanted to eat. He might be eating alone or with his siblings. Perhaps a child goes into the kitchen and decides what foods he wants to eat and then decides if he wants to eat in the bedroom, in front of the TV, or some other place. The parent and child are likely not eating together. The good news is a child in this environment isn't being pressured or forced to eat all of his food or a new food. On the other hand, a child in this mealtime environment is missing out on experiences that can build his life skills and eating capabilities and is missing out on experiences that build healthy emotional connection between him and you.

I think there can be a variety of reasons why this happens. One possibility is one or both parents in an unstructured mealtime environment want to see their child be happy. Thus, few or no limits are set with the child in order to prevent the child from being unhappy. This can also be an attempt by the parent to minimize the amount of stress in the family, especially if there is already enough stress in the rest of their lives.

Unstructured can also mean that the family is sitting together, but the parent is cooking different foods to cater to the specific likes and dislikes of each child. This ends up being a lot of work for the parent and can increase the parent's frustration and/or resentment. The focus of the mealtime has shifted to being whether the child is eating or not eating. In essence, the child's eating has become more important than the child and the child's overall development.

Now, before I go any further, I want to say something. Discussions about kids' eating and parents' feeding are an emotional topic and are emotional for a number of legitimate reasons. This topic can bring up feelings in a parent such as guilt, shame, and regret. I want you to know that at the core of my approach both in my work and in this book, I consciously try not to judge parents about their kids' eating or the parents' mealtime behaviors. My experience is nearly all parents want the best for their kids and are doing the best they can. My experience is a majority of parents have not been exposed to some or all of these strategies for building healthy mealtime environments. How could a parent possibly use a strategy if it wasn't used during the parent's childhood and the parent never learned about it from anyone else?

I also aim to support parents in providing a pattern of "good enough" parenting. I do not aim for perfect parenting. Trying to be a perfect parent is a set-up for self-hate and self-condemnation toward yourself and frustration with and rejection of others. It also makes the people around you miserable and makes you miserable. Perfect parenting focuses too much on the parent. Good enough parenting has a healthy balance by valuing the needs of the child and the needs of the parent. With good enough parenting, both the parent and the child are each genuinely important.

Rigid Mealtime Environment
So, let's go back to the different mealtime environments. Another extreme is the rigid mealtime environment. Families that have a rigid mealtime environment eat together but there is so much enforced structure that the mealtime environment has little joy, is usually tense, and is unpleasant. You might see behaviors such as children being told to eat all of the food on their plates, little in the way of spontaneous conversation, children fearing they will be reprimanded, and even no conversation.

In the rigid mealtime, the parent is using their power to set when and where their child will eat and for choosing what foods will be offered to their child. That's good. However, the parent may use their power to pressure or require their child to eat all of their food or to eat a food the child doesn't like. Children may not be allowed to talk except when allowed by the parent. It is likely a tense time and with little joy.

One or both parents in a rigid mealtime environment want their child to be obedient and/or to have self-control. The problem is that the strongest self-control you can build in a child is self-control you help the child build internally and self-control that is connected to your genuine love. Self-control you build in your child by having them obey what you tell them to do is actually compliance. Compliance is a weaker type of self-control and is not connected with genuine love.

In a rigid mealtime environment, you may interpret a child's refusal to eat all of their food or to eat a certain food as the child being disobedient. So the solution becomes stepping in and asserting control over the situation and becoming the enforcer at mealtime. Being the enforcer is unpleasant living for you (and for your child). This approach may achieve the outcome you want, but it isn't going to result in healthiest development for your child. It may give you a compliant child but not a more capable child.

Safe, Nurturing, and Developmentally Challenging Mealtime Environment

© Phyllis Meredith – www.phyllismeredith.com

I think there is a middle ground for mealtime environments that is emotionally and physically safe, nurturing, and yet developmentally challenging in a healthy way. It provides the kind of nurturing that builds healthy emotional connection, is pleasant, and is enjoyable. It also provides enough structure that your child feels safe and trusting. But, it becomes even more developmentally stronger by providing developmentally appropriate challenges that support your child's continuing development. If you find your mealtime has become unpleasant, chaotic, or stressful, then some changes are needed.

Jean Clarke and Connie Dawson point out in <u>Growing Up Again</u> that parenting is basically providing nurture and providing structure.[5] Setting the when, where, and what of mealtimes is one part of parental love. It is providing structure. Others call it setting limits or creating boundaries. The other part of parental love is nurture. Both are important and both are needed. Jean and Connie point out (p.8, 1989) that "having firm Structure makes it easier to deliver loving Nurture."

The unstructured mealtime does not have structure and may not have nurture. The rigid mealtime has structure but not much nurture. The emotionally safe, nurturing, and developmentally challenging mealtime has structure **and** nurture. Having both key parts of parental love makes this mealtime environment the most positive and strongest mealtime environment.

The safe, nurturing, and developmentally challenging mealtime environment focuses on building a child's eating capability and life skills. It also focuses on building a mealtime environment that provides healthy connection and provides developmentally appropriate challenges while providing appropriate support. The child matters enough to the parent for the parent to sit with the child. And the child is more important to the parent than the food, how much the child eats, or even whether or not the child eats a particular food.

The Experience of Each Mealtime Environment
So, what is each mealtime environment like for a child? For the parent?

Unstructured mealtime environment – the child and the parent miss out on an opportunity to gain or build some positive emotional connection with each other. The child may have a genuine feeling of loneliness even if he is preoccupied with TV or a computer game. He will miss out on opportunities to experience the challenge and discomfort of a new food. He will miss an opportunity to receive loving support from his parent as he deals with the challenge of the new food. The parent misses out on some opportunities to provide the kind of parenting that provides a deep satisfaction.

Rigid mealtime environment – the child misses out on an opportunity to learn that eating and sharing a pleasant meal with others is one of life's true joys. The child misses out on opportunities to build a healthy capability about eating enough to satisfy his hunger and then stopping. The child misses an opportunity to receive some positive emotional connection. The parent misses an opportunity to have mealtime be a relaxed, pleasant, enjoyable, and emotionally connecting time together. If a child is forced to eat all of their food or eat a food the child doesn't like, that is a terribly unpleasant experience for the child and is an experience that actually builds emotional disconnection. It provides the child with an experience of not receiving loving support. It is also an unpleasant experience for the parent.

<u>Safe, nurturing, and developmentally challenging mealtime environment</u> - the child receives an opportunity to learn that eating and sharing a pleasant meal is one of life's true joys. The child receives opportunities to build a healthy capability about eating enough to satisfy his hunger and then stopping. The child and the parent receive an opportunity to gain or build some positive emotional connectedness with each other. The parent receives some opportunities to provide the kind of parenting that provides a deep satisfaction. The child receives an opportunity to experience the challenge and discomfort of a new food along with receiving an opportunity to receive loving support from his parent as he deals with the challenge of the new food.

One Last Thought

As you work to change or strengthen your mealtime, there is a good chance that this will bring challenges to you. A challenge might be about your child, or it might be about yourself. As you work to create a more developmentally healthy mealtime environment for your child, you are really working to create a better life for your child. But, as you do this work, you may experience grief or sadness that comes from giving your child some love, care, and/or connection you didn't receive as a child. This opens the door for some genuine healing of some hurt from your own childhood.

As I have learned to welcome and accept a challenge in my life and then deal with the challenge, I have found there is always a gift on the other side of the challenge. The gift is usually more genuine peace, freedom, joy, or love. And those are wonderful gifts.

Also, as you start to adopt these new strategies, you are likely to encounter struggles/challenges with your child's eating. You may decide to step in and assert control over the situation and become the enforcer at mealtime. Or you may decide to make adjustments by doing whatever it takes to make your child happy. Being the enforcer is unpleasant living for you (and for your child). Doing whatever it takes to make your child happy can be tiring for you. And neither approach is going to result in healthiest development for your child.

Again, what can be particularly helpful for a parent is to find a Circle of Security Parenting© group so you can build some basic relationship capabilities that do a great job of ending a number of the entrenched relationship struggles a parent may have with their child, including struggles with connecting to each other.

I also highly recommend the Ages and Stages chapter in <u>Growing Up Again</u>. The chapter is very readable, very helpful, and to the point. It covers seven developmental stages from birth through early adulthood. It briefly lists the child's developmental tasks of each stage, typical behaviors of the child at that stage, helpful parenting behaviors, unhelpful parenting behaviors, and affirming messages your child needs to hear at this stage.

Then this chapter in <u>Growing Up Again</u> gets even better. The authors understand that no parent had a perfect childhood and that each parent was actually wounded as part of growing up. Their emphasis is on the fact our woundedness from the past affects our parenting today. They view struggles with parenting as a potential doorway to taking a closer look at our own woundedness. The authors do a superb job of listing clues that indicate a parent may have a need that needs to be addressed. They also list specific activities that can help and some loving, developmentally appropriate statements a parent can say to herself or himself.

The trick is to seek and to find the developmentally healthy middle ground and stay away from the two extremes. What I try to do in this book is help you find the developmentally healthy middle ground in regard to mealtimes. Hopefully, parenting will become easier and more satisfying.

Let's go to the next chapters and look at some specific strategies for building safe, nurturing, and developmentally challenging mealtimes.

Food for Thought

1. Can you think of a time when using your power at a meal allowed your child to have some power?

2. Why is it important for a parent to use their power to keep a mealtime emotionally safe?

3. How does allowing your child to have power support his/her healthy development?

4. Can you think of an instance in your childhood in which you were allowed or not allowed to have some power? How did that feel for you?

5. Do you think you are capable of offering your child broccoli for five years? Would you get frustrated? How might you deal with this frustration?

6. Do you know a family with an unstructured or rigid mealtime environment? What do you notice about their level of positive emotional connection during meals?

CHAPTER 4:

Experiencing the Joy of Having a Positive Emotional Connection with a Caring Parent

Have you ever had a frustration, concern, or worry in your life? A joy? Something interesting or funny happen to you?

If you had someone listen to you as you talked about your frustration, concern, worry, joy, or interesting experience, you often found you felt better after having shared about it with your friend. Being genuinely listened to reduces your stress, helps you have an insight or understanding, and/or provides a greater sense of emotional connection. Kids need the same experience.

I spoke with a group of ten moms about building healthy mealtime environments. After I shared about the four things fed at a mealtime, I asked them what got in the way of their kids receiving their love, care, and connection during a meal. They said having the TV on and their kids watching TV during the meal. I asked them if they would be willing to have one dinner with the TV turned off. They all agreed to try it. Their other assignment was just to observe everyone's reaction to having the TV off during dinner. We met several weeks later and eight of the ten moms were there. All of them reported turning the TV off during dinner. One mom reported she never had the TV on during meals anyway, but for the other seven moms, this was new behavior. Four moms said they learned things about their kids' lives that they likely would not have learned if the TV had been on. All of the moms shared that they felt that their kids had received more of their love, care, and connection. Several moms reported their kids asked why the TV was off and accepted the explanation. Two moms shared that each had an elementary school age child throw a temper tantrum due to the TV being off during dinner. One child proclaimed he was unable to eat unless the TV was on. We had not discussed at our first meeting how to handle kids getting upset with the parent for turning the TV off during dinner. Both moms reported telling their kids that this was the homework assignment they had been given, and they had to do it. After hearing that explanation both kids stopped their temper tantrums.

Sometimes, in our desire to see our children grow up and become more competent and capable, we can forget about a crucial and basic fact. Kids need the experience of having a positive emotional connection with a caring parent. They need it a lot, and they need it everyday. Actually, it is a universal need. Regardless of income and regardless of race, kids (and adults) need emotional connection.

Emotional connection provides comfort and reassurance to your child. It builds trust, a sense of emotional safety, a sense of being known, a sense of being cared for, and a sense of having someone on their side. These are great gifts for a child to receive. They help a child to become a braver explorer of her world because she has a secure base to leave as she explores and a safe haven to return to when she starts to feel overwhelmed in her exploring. This secure base and safe haven help make a child to grow and to become stronger and more resilient as she deals with each new challenge in her life.

University of Minnesota Connectedness Research

This study of over 36,000 7th-12th grade students focused on protective factors against the "quietly disturbed behaviors" (poor body image, disordered eating, etc.) and acting out behaviors (drug use, pregnancy risk, etc.).[6] The five variables included family connectedness, school connectedness, religious connectedness, low family stress, and age. These five variables "correctly classified 71.8% of adolescents, including close to 9 in 10 of those at low risk for quietly disturbed behaviors."

© Phyllis Meredith – www.phyllismeredith.com

One of the highlights was "adolescents could not be differentiated as low or high-risk for quietly disturbed and acting out behaviors on the basis of their families' socioeconomic status, after the preceding variables were taken into account."

Another highlight was "Measures of caring and connectedness surpassed demographic variables such as two parent vs. single parent family structure as protective factors against high risk behaviors."

The strongest protective factor was family connectedness. School connectedness was the second strongest protective factor. School connectedness was defined as enjoying school, and experiencing a sense of belonging and connectedness to school.

Family connectedness referred to a sense of belonging and closeness to family. It was defined as enjoying, feeling close to, and feeling cared for by family members. At the core of family connectedness is the adolescent's experience of being connected to at least one caring, competent adult in a loving, nurturing relationship.

Interestingly, when the results were analyzed after controlling for family connectedness, adolescents who on average ate dinner with their parents at least five times a week had less substance use, fewer depressive symptoms, and less suicide involvement, and better grades.[6]

So, it would be easy to say that family mealtimes are the answer. But, that is too simple of an answer. In fact, a 2012 article analyzed data related to the social and health benefits of family mealtimes from the National Longitudinal Survey of Adolescent Health.[7] Overall, how often a family is just having family meals did not hold up as having the effect on adolescents' well-being as has been touted. What actually seems to be important is the quality of family relationships.

However, mealtimes can be a very good place to start because it can be such a good and consistent place where families can be with one another and build genuine connection. Yet, I've spoken to a number of adults who had family mealtimes as they grew up, but they were family mealtimes that built emotional disconnection.

If it is painful to eat together, then family meals may not be the answer right away. In fact, it would be a hurtful answer. Yet, becoming aware of our own struggle, resistance, and pain around mealtimes is often a necessary step in order to reclaim mealtimes as a genuine place of emotional connection for your family.

The most important point for me from Resnick's study is connection matters and it matters quite a bit. The trick is to promote and support family mealtimes that are safe, trusting, nurturing, enjoyable, and developmentally challenging. That is what will build genuine and developmentally supportive connection.

The experiences of having a positive emotional connection with a caring parent need to happen enough so that the experiences become a pattern of experience.

When it becomes a pattern and then a consistent pattern of experience, the pattern helps build neural pathways in their brains. A wonderful book, A General Theory of Love, discusses how these patterns and resulting neural pathways create implicit memories.[8] Basically, an implicit memory is a belief that has been created from repeated experience. The belief helps to form what to expect from relationships and from the world. Since these beliefs are based on emotional and repeated experiences, they are quite powerful. What makes this even more interesting is that the belief may not be a conscious belief that one can easily articulate. Then it gets even more interesting, because we carry these beliefs with us into adulthood as a way of being and interacting in the world. In a sense, these beliefs are what create our expectations of others such as whether I expect I will receive help if I ask for help or whether I will be comforted if I am in need of comfort.

If you ever find yourself using a behavior that is destructive to yourself or limiting your life and you can't figure out why you keep repeating this behavior, there is a good chance this is an old belief at work. Beliefs are important because they can drive our behavior. Often times we aren't even aware we have a belief that is driving our behavior. One of the best arenas for uncovering a belief you have is with a struggle you are having with another person. Rather than attacking the person or getting angry or resentful toward the person, you need to take the time to sit with the struggle and make the effort to understand and articulate your underlying belief. That is the beginning of freedom for you.

So?

So, what does all of this have to do with mealtimes?

Well, it turns out that mealtimes can be a great place for your child to have these experiences of having a positive emotional connection with a caring parent. Let's look at why this is so.

First, having a parent sit with her at a meal gives a child the experience she is important enough to you for you to take the time to sit with her. You are giving the gift of your time and your presence.

Second, when a mealtime is emotionally safe and pleasant, you provide an oasis to your child. You are giving the gift of an emotionally safe place in her life and a place where she can relax and enjoy being with other people. These two gifts alone are huge, life-giving gifts to your child.

Third, when you ask questions about your child's day, you listen, and you are genuinely interested in what she has to say, you give a wonderful gift. The gift you give is that she matters to you. Being listened to and understood gives a child an experience of being seen, being known, and being accepted. She will store this experience in her heart.

Fourth, when you allow your child to share honestly about her struggles, you give the gift of having a safe and trusting place where she can reveal the challenges in her life. This also gives you the opportunity to show her you are on her side.

Fifth, when you allow your child to share the successes she had today, you are giving the gift of letting her share her genuine joy of success with someone who cares deeply for her.

Sixth, when you sense something is troubling your child, you can give your child the gift of having someone help her identify what is bothering her. You may end up taking action on your child's behalf that you would not have taken if you had not learned about your child's struggle.

Seventh, when you provide your child with experiences of positive emotional connection that also validates to a child that they exist to another person. This might seem a little ridiculous to you, but I think some kids, especially kids experiencing emotional neglect, can end up without many experiences that validate their existence. Additionally, as Circle of Security Parenting© points out, kids who receive delight from their parents and other important caregivers, especially a pattern of delight, end up with a greater sense of self worth.

When you create and maintain a mealtime environment that provides these relational experiences, you are being a powerful, loving, and kind parent. You are building a child with an internal sense she has genuine worth and a child with an internal sense of trust. You are building a child who has a joyful and genuine connection with others and knows in her heart that she matters. This is powerful, powerful parenting. Let me say this again. When you do this, you are providing powerful, powerful parenting. That is a truth about yourself you have a right to accept and own.

Food for Thought

1. What gets in the way of your child having a positive emotional connection during a meal?

2. How does routine emotional connectedness promote a child's self-esteem?

3. How would your family react to a "no electronics during mealtime rule?" How would you react?

4. The author states at the end of the chapter "When you create and maintain a mealtime environment that provides these relational experiences, you are being a powerful, loving, and kind parent." What is your response to this statement?

CHAPTER 5:

Learning to Say No (and experience still being loved)

I came across the following delightful story of a mom, Muriel Hastings, from the Seattle, Washington area.

Years ago, when my daughter was a pre-teen, she was involved with a local and somewhat famous girls' chorus. As a parent I was doing everything I could to support my blossoming songbird of a child, but I always felt a bit uneasy about the chorus director. Something about him made me uneasy, so I kept a close eye on the almost daily practice sessions. When the time came for a big performance in a cathedral space, I attended the rehearsals. And I witnessed the chorus director bully and belittle the girls. I watched the parents around me sit mutely. I became agitated and enraged, and in an overpowering need to protect my child and ALL of the other children (whose parents were mute), I stood up in the middle of the cathedral, stopped the rehearsal and in a voice that I barely recognized as my own, I said, "You will NOT be permitted to shame and belittle these children. I am taking my child out of this rehearsal and this organization, and I suggest that the rest of you save your own children from this bully!" Hundreds of parents, one by one, began to applaud, then there was a standing ovation. My daughter wasn't sure if she should be embarrassed or proud. But she followed me out of the cathedral as did a number of other parents with their own daughters in tow.[9]

I like what Muriel did very much. She is an adult who has the life skill of being able to say No. In this case she said No on her daughter's behalf. But, she also said No on her own behalf. And she said No on behalf of the other children in the girls' choir.

Being able to say No can help protect you or protect someone you love. It is a valuable and essential life skill for an adult to have. It is also a valuable and essential life skill for a child to have. Like any life skill, it has to be practiced enough so it has some strength about it and has to be supported so your child knows he has your support to use it.

But, let's look at this from another angle. Do you know an adult who cannot say No to other people? What is their life like? When I do presentations with parents and preschool teachers and pose this question, I get different responses.

Most adults tell me they do know another adult who cannot say No to other people. Then we talk about what they have noticed about the lives of people who can't say No to other people. Some people share that the person's life is chaotic or is a mess. Others share about how they are so busy doing things for other people that they often are resentful or stressed out. There is usually not a spirit of joy about them. Others have shared that people who can't say No are more likely to hang out with unsafe or dangerous people who may harm them or harm their kids.

An adult who cannot say No in their life is much more likely to let someone else run their life. That can be a disaster for the person and for their kids too. Even dangerous to them.

Then we talk about whether being able to say No is a good life skill for their kids. Most adults agree that it is. They also agree that helping their child be able to say No helps their child be successful in life.

Then we list the things a child might need to be able to say No to. A child may need to say No to someone hurting them or someone wanting the child to do something that isn't good for the child. The child might need to be able to say No to inappropriate touch, drugs, or other things.

Yet, for any skill to be developed and strengthened, it needs to be practiced. What makes it a stronger skill is when a parent supports their child for saying No.

But what makes it a quite powerful skill is when your child can say No, receive your support for saying No, <u>and</u> experience still being loved by you after saying No. For the child, that experience is one of being able say No and experiencing still being loved. This is a powerful gift from you to your child. Let me say this again, this is a powerful gift from you to your child.

You want your child to be able to say No when it is developmentally appropriate to say No. I am not saying to support your child every time he says No; only the times when it is developmentally appropriate. There are times when your child will actually need to receive No from you instead. That is covered in the next chapter.

<u>Mealtimes and Learning to Say No (and still be loved)</u>
The good news is being able to say No is a life skill that can be developed. An early, important, and frequent place where you can help build this important life skill is at mealtimes. Of course, it is not as simple as just having a meal together. That is an essential part. But the other essential part is what you allow and how you react.

Mealtimes can be great opportunities for a child to develop the life skill of learning to say No. But what makes it powerful is for the child to be able to say No and also experience being loved.

So, how does this work at mealtimes?

<u>Appetite</u>
Several factors have a role to play. Obviously, a key factor is the level of your child's appetite since that can and will vary. Another is who gets to be the expert about and who gets to be in charge of your child's appetite. So, let's talk first about appetite.

The thing you want to keep in mind is that a child's appetite can vary from meal to meal and meal to snack. A child may eat a large amount of food at one meal and a small amount at the next meal. Or just the opposite. And that is normal. It may be puzzling to you or frustrating to you, but your child is still being normal.

A key part about appetite is ownership. Who has ownership of a child's appetite? Who does the child's appetite belong to? A key point for a parent who wants to keep their sanity is to remember a child's appetite is their appetite. You are not in charge of a child's appetite. It doesn't belong to you. Nor does it belong to any other adult or child.

A child's appetite is their tool. As a parent, you do your best work when you help your child become aware of this tool and help them learn to use this tool. Your goal is to help your child gain confidence and strength in their natural ability to be aware of their appetite, accept it as it is, and use it to guide him about how much to eat and when to stop eating. In a way, it is helping your child become aware of a force within himself – his appetite - and then learning to use this force in his life rather than being controlled by this force

A child's appetite can vary from other children and reflect their uniqueness. Kids in the same family can also vary. One may need more calories per pound of weight than their brother or sister does.

Your child's appetite may also increase due to having a growth spurt or because of an increase in physical activity.

Your child's appetite may decrease after a growth spurt is over or decrease due to an illness. Possibly, and unknown to you, your child has had a snack in the past hour.

What is challenging for a parent is the fact the parent cannot look at their child and know how much their child will need to eat at a meal or snack.

The second key concept is who is the expert on the level of your child's appetite? Is it you or is it your child? Just like you are the expert about the level of your appetite at a meal, your child is the expert of his level of appetite at a meal. You are not the expert about the level of your child's appetite.

So, what genuine challenge does this present to you as a parent? Your challenge is whether or not you will choose to trust your child as the expert of his appetite. If you find that you cannot allow yourself to trust your child as the expert of his appetite, don't judge yourself because there is likely a very good reason why you cannot. However, I do encourage you to get help about your difficulty in trusting your child as the expert of his appetite. Getting help will be a huge gift for your child and a huge gift for you.

So, then, what is your job as the child's parent?

Basically, your job is to accept, trust, and support. Keep in mind, whatever his appetite; your child still needs your love, your care, and your connection.

How Your Child Says No
Letting your child choose to eat some of his food, not eat at all, or not eat a particular food you have offered is allowing your child to say No. He may say No by not eating, by shaking his head, or by using words. All 3 ways are his ways of saying No.

A child will naturally say No about not eating all of his food or a particular food. That is normal behavior for a child. The key action is his parent's reaction. Will you accept his No or reject it? Will you trust him about his appetite or his reaction to a food or not trust him? Will you support him in a developmentally supportive way or focus on getting your way?

3 Key Themes: Acceptance vs. Rejection; Trust vs. Distrust; and Providing Support vs. Getting Your Way

At times, your child will have little or no appetite at a meal and tell you he is not hungry or just not eat much of his food. He is doing good work by paying attention to and accepting what his body is telling him about his appetite, trusting what his appetite tells him, and communicating this honestly to you.

The key action here is whether you will accept what he is communicating to you, especially when he has little or no appetite.

You may not accept what he communicates to you about his appetite. You may decide you know what is best for him and pressure him to eat his food or get mad at him for not eating his food. What you think he should do then becomes more important to you than you trusting him. It turns into a battle of wills.

When this happens, you give your child an experience. His experience is "If I say No, I will pay a price for saying No." He experiences having his No being overridden. He experiences a negative emotional interaction with you. He experiences emotional disconnection and misses an opportunity to have an experience of positive emotional connection. Rather than acceptance, he is receiving rejection.

Another interaction I have come across is a parent withdrawing emotionally from her child when the child doesn't want to eat a food that is special to the parent or a food the parent has lovingly prepared. The parent takes it personally. Again, the child learns he pays a price by saying No.

The question to ask yourself is, "Can I trust that my child will get enough food if I let him be in charge of how much he eats at a meal or snack?" I don't ask this to judge you, but to consider whether or not you struggle with trusting your child's eating capability.

Your job is simply to provide regular and predictable opportunities for your child to eat and provide enough food so your child can get all the food he needs. Having done this, your job is to trust or learn to trust that your child will get enough to eat to grow and to maintain his genetically endowed body size.

A good question to ask yourself is, "Am I making the food more important than my child?"

Keep in mind your love, care, and connection are more important than any food and are more important than how much your child eats at a meal. If you can use this approach, you will be giving a wonderful and developmentally supportive gift to your child. If you are encountering a struggle about your child's eating, a kind thing to do is just ask yourself this question and, in a low key way and hopefully without judgment, just observe yourself and your reaction to your child.

Of course, how much your child eats is not the whole story. Another part of your job is providing your child with developmentally appropriate challenges that promote healthy developmental growth by offering him new foods. That is covered in chapter seven.

Other Thoughts

Some parents are uncomfortable with letting their child say No. This may be a major shift in how you parent. I think the trick is to decide whether or not your child will receive any developmental gifts that contribute to him being successful in life by allowing him to say No about how much he eats or to eating a new food right away.

Another important reason is letting your child say No can bring up issues from your own childhood. Perhaps you weren't allowed to say No about having to eat all of the food on your plate or having to eat a new food you didn't like. Or, perhaps you did say No and experienced being treated in an unloving way. It is quite possible you made a vow then that you would never treat your kids that way when you grew up.

These were strong and emotionally disconnecting experiences that left a powerful impact on you. They wounded you about trust, emotional safety, emotional connection, and how to face and deal with a challenge with loving support. My experience is you can avoid facing these old wounds, but that doesn't heal them nor does it reduce their power over you in your life. And until they are acknowledged and addressed they will interfere will your parenting and your child's healthy development.

When a child has the pattern of a mealtime environment in which he is pressured to eat all of his food or a new food, that produces emotional disconnection. Yet, when a child has the pattern of the other mealtime environment extreme of not having a parent sit with him that also produces emotional disconnection. Your goal is actually a mealtime environment pattern that stays in the developmentally healthy middle ground that builds emotional connection and stays away from the extremes that build emotional disconnection.

By the way, as you are able to provide your child a healthier mealtime environment than you experienced as a child, give yourself credit. Specifically, you can give yourself credit for being generous because you have made the effort to give your child something better than you received as a child. That is huge and very loving.

Keep in mind it can be emotionally painful when you first give your child a more loving type of parenting than you received as a child. It can also break your heart because as you give it, you start to realize in your heart what you missed as a child. Just keep in mind that giving your genuine love is a powerful act of love and can be as redemptive for your child as it is for you.

Food for Thought

1. What was your reaction to Muriel saying No to the chorus director?

2. Do you think being able to say No is an important life skill? Why or why not?

3. What is your response to letting your child be in charge of how much he or she eats?

4. If you allow your child to be in charge of how much he or she eats at a meal, does that make parenting a little easier? Why or why not?

5. Are there any experiences from your own childhood that might get in the way of letting your child be in charge of how much he or she eats?

CHAPTER 6:

Learning to Receive No
(and experience still being loved)

Have you ever had a friend listen to you share about a difficult situation you went through and then say something back to you which let you know she understood in her heart what you experienced? It leaves you feeling quite good. Your friend:

- Listened to you.

- Believed you.

- Understood you.

The way you shared, and your friend listened, gave you an experience that built:

- A sense of emotional safety.

- Trust.

- Emotional connection.

My experience is I have a greater sense of genuine aliveness after having such an experience.

You can provide your child with similar experiences when you first set a limit with your child. What this chapter covers are the developmental gifts you give your child when you set limits with your child that are developmentally appropriate. This chapter also covers how you can do this in such a way that it actually becomes powerful parenting. I believe a child who receives No in a way that leaves the child still feeling loved receives a powerful gift.

Kids who do not receive developmentally appropriate limits are missing out on some important opportunities that will support their healthy development. One preschool teacher shared with me about a four year old in her class who was asked by his mom every afternoon when she picked him up what he wanted for dinner. The child would say he wanted a Happy Meal from McDonald's. The teacher said this had been happening every day for two years. The teacher also shared that the child had been getting a Happy Meal for dinner each night for the past two years.

I joked with the other preschool teachers and said, "When this child grows into an adult, would you want to be married to him?" No one said yes, and we talked about the likelihood that as an adult he would likely have an expectation he could get what he wants when he wants it. That sort of expectation can be a huge barrier to developing a trusting and genuinely caring relationship in a marriage.

What is clear to me is this mother genuinely wanted her child to be happy. There is nothing wrong with wanting your child to be happy. However, the child was missing some opportunities with someone who loves him to experience not getting his way, learning to communicate his displeasure, and then learning to experience being loved even as a limit is set and maintained.

The key point is that setting a limit with your child can be an act of genuine love. Failing to set a limit with your child can be an act of shortchanging your child of your genuine love.

So, how does limit setting occur around mealtimes? The limit might be telling your child she cannot have a snack because you're serving dinner in 30 minutes. Your limit might be telling your child this is what we've having for dinner and not fixing a separate dinner for your child. Or your limit might be about letting your child know her behavior at the table is inappropriate and not acceptable.

These actions by a parent give your child a developmentally appropriate challenge. Whcn I do presentations with parents, I usually say at this point, "And of course your child will stand up, start clapping, and say 'Thank you for setting a limit with me and supporting my healthy development.'" In our dreams.

The No
When you set a limit by saying, "No you can't have a snack now because we're having dinner in 30 minutes," your child will not be pleased, especially if this is a new limit you are setting. Perhaps you used to give your child a snack whenever she wanted it.

Most likely, your child will do a great job of communicating how upset she is about this limit and use her favorite strategies to get you to give her what she wants. She will likely try to get you to change back to the old way you used to do things.

Your child wants you to change your No to Yes. By the way, that is completely normal. So, she pushes back. She says she needs to eat right now. She says her stomach is hurting her. She says she is starving. She says you're mean. She might say "I don't love you." Then, she'll play her ace of spades; she'll say "You don't love me." All of this is to get you to give in and give her what she wants.

Your job now is to maintain the boundary you set and not give in to your child. This can be hard and challenging work.

© Phyllis Meredith – www.phyllismeredith.com

Parents vary in their ability to set limits such as these. And usually for very good reasons. You may have a deep desire for your child to be happy and not want to make your child unhappy by setting a limit with her. It may make you uncomfortable to set a limit with your child. Your child may be gifted in getting you to change your mind after you initially set a limit.

The problem is children need to receive limits. Limits give them an opportunity to express their unhappiness about another person's decision. Limits give your child a developmentally appropriate struggle. Limits give your child an opportunity for a deeper level of emotional connection. Limits also help your child learn she will not always get her own way. Limits help your child feel emotionally safe.

Another important reason is the act of setting a limit with your child can bring up issues from your own childhood. Maybe no one set limits with you. That was an experience of being neglected. In a sense that was an experience of you experiencing a predictable pattern of having no one to say No to you. Maybe inconsistent limits were set with you. You had the experience of someone sometimes setting appropriate limits with you, but it was an unpredictable pattern of setting limits. Perhaps you had the experience of limits being set harshly and without any love.

<u>Giving the No</u>
Most kids (ok, all kids) do not like to have their parents say No when the kid asks their parent to do something for them.

Learning to receive No is a life skill all children need when they are in school, when they have jobs, and when they are trying to make a relationship work.

An adult who cannot receive No from another person is going to be an unpleasant person to be with, work with, and will have serious struggles in maintaining a healthy, loving, and generous relationship with another person.

In order for a child to receive No, you have to first give them your No. At its heart, it can be an act of genuine love for someone to say No to us. They may say it for our protection, for their protection, or for our continued growth as a person.

In fact, the most loving action for a parent to take sometimes is to say No. For example, telling a four-year-old child that the child cannot have a snack because dinner will be served in 30 minutes is an act of genuine love. By not allowing the child to have a snack, you help your child come to the meal with a good appetite. You also help your child to have a feeling of being hungry for 30 minutes, learn she can survive the feeling, and learn she is stronger than her feeling of hunger.

So, it is important for a child to receive a No from you when it is appropriate to give a No. However, you can give your child your No in a way that builds emotional disconnection which causes your child to not feel loved. Let's look at that.

The Two Extremes and the Developmentally Healthy Middle
Let's look at what the two extremes are and what the developmentally healthy middle looks like.

One extreme is to never or hardly ever set a limit with your child by saying No. Instead, you let your child do what they want or give them what they want. Some parents struggle with saying No to their child's request. The earlier vignette of the child who requested and received a McDonald's Happy Meal everyday for dinner is an example of one extreme.

The other extreme is saying No but doing it in a harsh or uncaring way that does not result in the child still feeling loved by you. You do good work by saying No, but you can also do it in a way that causes emotional disconnection between you and your child. That is, both of you end up having some emotional disconnection. As a result, this type of limit setting is not emotionally satisfying for you or for your child.

The developmentally healthy middle is saying No **and** also saying things that let your child know you understand what she wants and what she is feeling.

The Push Back
When a parent says No to their child, the child does not break into a big smile, start clapping her hands, and say "Thanks mom (or thanks dad) for being such a loving parent by setting a limit with me." Instead,

your child will try to get you to change your mind and do what she wants. She will push back. That is normal. As Drs. Henry Cloud and John Townsend shared in their book, <u>Boundaries with Kids</u>, "The trick of parenting is to hold onto your limit one more time than your children hold onto the demand. That's all you need – one more."[10]

Keep in mind you are giving your child an opportunity to push back. This is good and strong parenting. You want a child who pushes back and is comfortable pushing back. There will be many occasions in your child's life, including her adult years, where she will need to push back.

Essentially, the parent just needs to say No one more time than the child pushes back. This is actually good parenting. But, as my friend Cheryl Alto states, it can also be lonely parenting because your limit has brought a separation into your relationship with your child.

So, let's look at how you can make it powerful parenting and heal the separation in your relationship with your child.

<u>Maintaining Emotional Connection</u>
Some parents find it difficult to set a limit with their child. Other parents find it easy to set a limit but do so in a way that doesn't build emotional connection. The trick is to use the limit setting as an opportunity, not to make your child happy, but to provide a limit <u>and</u> to provide an interaction that promotes emotional connection. Your goal is to achieve both outcomes.

Providing the limit gives your child a challenge. That is why you want the challenge to be developmentally appropriate. You want the challenge to be something she can handle but not so big that it is overwhelming for her. Telling your four-year-old to she will have to wait 30 minutes until she can eat dinner is giving her a developmentally <u>appropriate</u> challenge.

Providing lunch to a four-year-old but not providing a snack 2½-3 hours later and having her wait until dinner to eat again is a developmentally

<u>inappropriate</u> challenge. It is expecting her to wait far too long until she eats again.

The key point is after you provide the limit and your child pushes back, you maintain the limit. You also want your child to have the experience of someone being on her side as she deals with the challenge you gave her.

Let's suppose your nine-year-old had a mid-afternoon snack but wants another snack 30 minutes before dinner. You tell her she will have to wait 30 minutes and dinner will be ready then. She may accept this. But let's assume she doesn't.

She will push back and try to get you to change your decision and give her a snack now. She will use her tools to get you to change – her anger, her persistence, her temper tantrum, her crying, her losing it, etc.

Your job is to maintain the limit as your child pushes back. Keep in mind that this is good parenting. But, this also becomes an opportunity to provide your child with an experience of powerful parenting. Thus, your first task is to set and then maintain the limit you set.

Your next task has two parts. You want to communicate:

1. You understand what your child is wanting.

2. You also want your child to know you understand the feelings she is having, which is showing genuine empathy.

It might look like this:

- <u>Child</u> – I'm hungry. I need to eat right now.

- <u>You</u> – Your stomach is telling you how hungry you are. It is uncomfortable to be so hungry. We will be having lunch in 30 minutes.

- <u>Child</u> – You don't understand. I'm really hungry. My stomach hurts.

- <u>You</u> – You are so hungry! It is making your stomach hurt! I know you want to eat right now. It really is hard to be so hungry. We will be eating in 30 minutes, and there will be plenty of food for you.

© Phyllis Meredith – www.phyllismeredith.com

You let your child know you understand she has feelings about receiving your limit. And you let her know what you think she is feeling. This gives your child a huge gift of emotional connection as she reacts to the limit you set. Essentially, you have provided her an experience of receiving No from you and still being loved, even after she reacts to your No.

Of course, this will not be a magical encounter where you say these things and your child looks up at you, smiles, and says thank you for being so caring and empathic to me and for setting such good developmental boundaries with me because you care so deeply about my healthy development. One mom shared with me that at this point she will bring her child into the kitchen to help which gives her child something to do and distracts her from her hunger.

You are letting your child know you understand she has feelings about receiving your limit. This helps your child keep a good emotional connection with you.

The Developmental Gifts to Your Child

There are a number of capabilities and developmentally supportive gifts your child will receive by this kind of parenting:

- Learning to live with some feelings of mild hunger for a short period of time. When this happens over and over your child learns she can tolerate and live with this feeling of mild hunger. That is building your child's ability to self-regulate herself and to strengthen her resilience.

- Learning that you really do mean it when you say she can only eat at meals and snacks and not in between.

- Learning she can receive your No, push back against you, and then be treated in a way that lets her know that she is loved. That deepens her emotional connection with you.

- Your child is much more likely to come to a meal or snack with a good appetite. A child who is hungry is more likely to try a new food and to enjoy the food you are offering.

- Learning to adjust her behavior to the limits she is coming to expect from you. Parents tell me that after they start practicing the structured times for meals and snacks and don't allow their kids to eat in between, they notice that their kids will go ahead and eat some even when not very hungry because their child has learned that if she doesn't eat some she will have to wait until the next scheduled snack or meal.

The Developmental Gifts to You

• Knowing that you are doing powerful parenting by setting developmentally appropriate limits and providing the type of interaction that lets your child know she is genuinely loved.

• Knowing that you are supporting your child's healthy development by setting and then maintaining the limit.

• Knowing that you are building positive emotional connection with your child.

By the way, the best book I've ever encountered about setting limits with kids is Boundaries with Children by Henry Cloud and John Townsend. Another book I like a lot is Raising Self-Reliant Children in a Self-Indulgent World by Stephen Glenn and Jane Nelson.[11]

Food for Thought

1. How do appropriate limits help your child's healthy development?

2. How important is emotional connection for a child? How does emotional connection support your child's healthy development?

3. Is it really possible for your child to experience an emotional connection with you even when you set and keep a limit with him or her?

4. Can you think of a time when someone set a limit with you but did it in a way that maintained emotional connection with you? How about a time when someone set a limit with you but did it in a way that damaged your emotional connection?

CHAPTER 7:

Learning to Deal with a Small Challenge (but with loving support)

Before posing two questions to you, I want to share the experience a mom shared with me about offering broccoli to her child.

This mom shared how she offered her three-year-old daughter broccoli by serving a small amount on her daughter's plate. Guess what happened? Her daughter wasn't interested and didn't try it. What was interesting was the mom did not pressure her daughter to eat the broccoli and did not turn it into a battle. In fact the mom stayed neutral, and she stayed low key. She offered broccoli the next night, got the same response, and stayed neutral and low key. The same thing happened the next night. The mom told me that she did the same thing for six nights in a row. On the 6th night her daughter finally decided on her own to try the broccoli. The mom reported that her daughter liked it.

What was going on in this situation was something much more important than whether or not the child ate the broccoli. This is a superb example of a mother offering a challenge and also providing her loving support.

Before we explore this issue further, let's step back from the broccoli and look at it from a developmental perspective.

But, first I have two questions for you:

1. In the past year have you had a challenge in your life? It could be a challenge with finances, a relationship, a car, or a number of other things.

2. Was it easier dealing with the challenge on your own or dealing with it while having the loving support of someone on your side?

I bring this up because each of us, whether we are a young infant, toddler, preschooler, child, teenager, young adult, or older adult will encounter challenges throughout our lives. Each challenge is an opportunity for growth or an opportunity to avoid growth. There are gifts we receive when we face and deal with a challenge. If we don't receive a challenge or we avoid a challenge, we don't receive the gifts. And we don't grow as a person.

Key Point: Providing your child with a challenge is not being a bad parent. It is being a good parent. However, providing a challenge and also giving your loving support is being a powerful parent.

A key part of parenting is finding the developmentally healthy middle ground. One extreme is to parent so your child faces as few challenges as possible. The other extreme is to parent so your child faces numerous challenges on his own, including challenges beyond his capability to handle them. Neither of those ways builds the most capable child and neither results in a child who has the most genuine love of learning.

The developmentally healthy middle ground is to parent in a way that offers your child developmentally appropriate challenges and loving support. A developmentally appropriate challenge is a challenge that is achievable by your child but not so big of a challenge that it is beyond your child's capability.

A key part of any challenge is the feeling of discomfort. The discomfort, if it is not too large or overwhelming, helps fuel the effort needed to face and deal with the challenge. However, as a parent, it can sometimes be emotionally difficult to watch your child face and deal with a challenge. You may even try to avoid your own discomfort by making sure your child has fewer challenges in his life.

Your loving support is what helps your child tolerate their feelings of discomfort and to persevere. Keep in mind that kids are created with an internal desire to grow in capability. Your loving support helps keep your child's feelings of discomfort from overpowering his internal desire to grow in capability. Part of a parent's job is having an expectation their child truly does have an inner drive to face and successfully deal with new challenges. But, your loving support during times of challenge is absolutely critical to building your child's capacity to handle challenges.

So?

So, what does this have to do with mealtimes? The primary way you provide your child with challenges is providing an environment where he will encounter challenges. A developmentally healthy mealtime environment will offer challenges to your child, but it will also offer loving support that helps your child successfully deal with the challenge and deal with it at a pace that is right for him.

If you go back to the Circle of Security® drawing of the Circle in chapter one, that journey around the Circle is being played out. One can view mealtimes as a time of exploration. And with any occasion when a child is exploring, the exploring can bring on a challenge. He may be exploring rules of behavior, relationship interactions, a new food, etc. Things may be going smoothly, or your child may be encountering a challenge. At that point, if he now experiencing some distress from the challenge, he needs his parent to realize he is at the bottom of the Circle. When the parent can recognize their child is at the bottom of the Circle and then determine what their child needs (protection, comfort, delight, or help organizing their feelings), and then provide what is needed, that reduces the stress the child is experiencing from the challenge. This loving support from his parent then makes the challenge manageable and helps restore the child to wanting to explore again. Most people will agree that challenge produces growth. But, I think challenge with connection and support produces the best and strongest growth in a child.

Exploration can result in distress. That is normal. But, what is really important is having someone Bigger, Stronger, Wiser, and Kind be there for you in your distress and restore you to feeling emotionally safe and secure. Joanne Brown, a colleague of mine in Canada, talks about kids needing co-regulation in order to develop self-regulation. A child experiencing distress and then having someone help him deal with his distress so he feels emotionally safe and secure is having an experience of co-regulation. In turn, a pattern of co-regulation will help to build the child's ability to self-regulate. Over time, our ability to self-regulate can become stronger and stronger, but, we never make it, even as adults, to a place where we can fully self-regulate. There will always be challenges, particularly novel challenges or overwhelming challenges, when we need another adult to provide some co-regulation.

Most people find it easier to deal with a challenge in their life when they have the loving support of a friend. It helps to have someone to support you, be on your side, and encourage you without pressuring you. It is a great feeling to have someone's loving support while facing a challenge.

For example, when you offer your child a new food you are giving your child a small challenge. You also have an opportunity to provide loving support to your child as they face their challenge. Giving your child a developmentally appropriate challenge is an act of love. Doing that and providing loving support is a powerful act of love.

Your child learns through experience to handle a small challenge on their own and at their own pace, which provides a genuine sense of accomplishment. Your child also learns by experience that a good strategy when handling a challenge is to have the loving support of someone.

What does the loving support look like at mealtimes?

- You sit with your child at the meal. Your presence is a crucial form of loving support.

- You use your power by deciding what foods will be offered, including foods new or nearly new to your child.

- You place a small amount of the new food on your child's plate. You are providing a challenge by placing some of the food on his plate, but you provide loving support by giving just a small amount which keeps it as a small challenge.

- You offer the new food neutrally (no pressure, no praise, and no reward). You give loving support by being neutral because this allows your child's eating to be 100% his business by not making his eating your business. If your child eats it, you stay low key. If your child tries it, you stay low key. If your child doesn't like it, you stay low key.

- You encourage your child to try a small amount, but you don't make or pressure your child eat it. You are providing loving support by encouraging your child to try the food, but you keep it low key by genuinely letting him have the power to decide whether or not to try it. It is also helpful if your child can observe you eating the food and enjoying it. That is why I encourage parents to serve new foods that they enjoy. It can be reassuring for a child to see you eat and enjoy a food that is new to your child.

- You allow your child to have and use their power about whether or not to eat the new food after trying it. Keep in mind your child has been acting bravely and with an intent to explore when he has tried a small amount of a new food. Taking a risk by tasting a new food has the potential to be an emotionally unpleasant experience for him. He needs the freedom, your permission, and your blessing to use his power and stop at this point. That allows him to stop this experience when it is a brief and mildly unpleasant experience and is only somewhat emotional. You've allowed him to use his power by taking a risk when he was ready, and you've allowed him to use his power to stop it before it became too unpleasant.

The simplest way to give a way out is to provide a paper napkin and teach your child how to politely place the food in the napkin if he doesn't like the food. You are giving your loving support by teaching your child a skill to handle a food he doesn't like <u>this time</u>. You are also giving loving support by giving your child your permission to not like a food this time and giving your permission to your child to take action to remove a food he doesn't like this time from his mouth. You are also giving loving support to your child by making your child more important than the food. You might say something like:

"That is great that you were adventurous by trying that food. It was also great that you stopped eating it when you didn't like it. Sometimes I have to try a new food a bunch of times before I learn to like it. I liked how brave you were to try it."

I always encourage parents to model using this strategy with the napkin in front of their kids. Your example gives strong permission to your child to use this strategy. Sharing your reaction to the food is also a chance for you to show your child appropriate language to use when you don't like a food. A parent using this strategy after trying and not liking food this time gives the parent a chance to say "I haven't learned to like it yet, but I plan to try it again and see if I like it then."

- You teach your child to use an acceptable statement to communicate he doesn't like it. Rather than letting your child say "Yuck" or "I hate this," you teach your child to use another statement. For instance, you might teach your child to say "This is interesting, but I don't think I want any more of it today." You are giving loving support by communicating your expectation that rude statements aren't allowed at your table. You are building your child's capability by teaching acceptable statements to use. You're also teaching your child how to contribute to keeping an emotionally safe, pleasant, and enjoyable mealtime environment.

- You talk about your child's experience. You might ask if it was different than he expected. You might say in a low key way that you admire him for being brave enough to try it.

- You offer a new food a number of times. This provides lots of <u>low stress opportunities</u> to see, smell, touch, and taste the new food, which are important steps in learning to like a new food.

Dr. Leeann Birch and her colleagues found that exposing a child to a new food by placing some of the new food on their plate helps the child learn to eat a new food.[12] But what made a much bigger difference was the child tasting the new food. In this particular case seven novel fruits (e.g. canned figs, canned lychee, and sugar palm) were offered.

When a child tasted a new food, the child was not required to swallow the food. As the number of times increased that kids saw the food on their plate or tasted the new food, the likelihood the child would prefer that food increased. However, it increased much more when the child tasted the food than when the child just had it on their plate but didn't try it. The kids had up to 15 exposures to each food. Basically, the more exposure and the more times a child tasted the food, the more likely the child was to prefer the food. However, the results were best when there were at least 10 exposures to the new food.

In a national random survey of over 3,000 primary caregivers, mostly mothers, nearly 25% of the parents reported they stop offering a new food if they thought their child didn't like the new food after offering it 1-2 times.[13] An additional 50% of the parents would stop offering the new food after 3-5 tries if they thought their child didn't like the new food. So, part of a parent's job is to provide plenty of exposures to a new food and to encourage their child to taste the food. You may actually need to offer a new food 10-15 times. Yes, you heard me correctly; 10-15 times.

Jane Wardle and her colleagues reported a similar experiment in 2003, but they focused on vegetables.[14] Their study worked with 156 parents of 2–6 year old children and focused on "increasing children's liking for a previously disliked vegetable." A taste test was used at the beginning to identify the 'target' vegetable for each child. The target vegetable could be carrots, cucumbers, tomatoes, celery, green pepper, or red pepper.

One group of parents gave their child a taste of this vegetable daily for 14 days. The children were also allowed to record their reaction to the food each day by choosing from three small "face" stickers - like, okay, or dislike. The face was placed into a colorful "vegetable diary" that had a row for each day to record the child's reaction.

Another group of parents were given nutritional advice and a leaflet promoting increased consumption of fruit and vegetables. A third group served as a control group and received no other intervention after the initial taste test. All participants took part in a post-intervention taste test.

The group of kids whose parent offered them a taste of their "target vegetable" daily for 14 days had the highest increases in liking and voluntarily eating their "target' vegetable" from pre- to post-intervention. The percentage of children in this group who voluntarily ate the "target vegetable" increased from 47% (pre-intervention) to 77% (post-intervention). In the group of kids whose parents just received information, the percentage of children who voluntarily ate the "target vegetable" increased from 45% to 60%. In the third group that served as the control group, the percentage of children who voluntarily ate the "target vegetable" decreased from 55 to 50%.

Nearly 30% of children in the group of parents who offered the "target vegetable" daily for 14 days ranked their target vegetable as the most liked. Whereas only 2% of the kids whose parents were given nutritional advice and a leaflet promoting increased consumption of fruit and vegetables group ranked their target vegetable as the most liked. 5% of the control group ranked their target vegetable as the most liked.

In the group of parents that offered the "target vegetable" daily for 14 days, seven out of ten parents surveyed felt that the intervention had had a lasting effect on their child's liking for the target vegetable. They said such things as: "…it is his favorite and he would not touch it before." Many parents from this group reported that their child had enjoyed the daily tasting of their "target vegetable" and that this had increased willingness to try other foods. One parent stated: "…it has made food more fun." Parents also reported: "…afterwards he kept asking to try other things." A number of parents said their participation in the 14 day intervention inspired them to: "be more adventurous in what I offer him." These statements by parents are statements reflecting deeper connection. My hunch is one reason this intervention succeeded so well is it also provided and supported more opportunities for connection between the mothers and their children. That is very developmentally savvy.

These are excellent results. My hunch is these parents will continue with their new mealtime behaviors because they saw a growth in their child's eating capability, an increase in their child's willingness and even desire to try other new foods, and an increase in their child enjoying the meal. These are big payoffs for parents. The design of this approach, which has the child choose the "face" sticker representing their true reaction to the food that day, allows the child the experience of having and using power. The instructions for the parent about what to say and do to encourage but not force the child to eat the vegetable and to not reward the child if he ate it allowed the child to experience still being loved after he used his power to eat or not eat the food and have his honest reaction to the food.

By the way, these researchers have made a tasting game kit, Tiny Tastes, available for purchase so you can use this approach with your children. It has a booklet, "face" stickers, and a link to an online instructional video. Just go to http://weightconcern.org.uk/node/302 to learn more about Tiny Tastes and to order the kit.

Additionally, give yourself credit for offering a new food at your family's mealtime. You've made your kids' lives a bit more interesting. You've brought some novelty into their lives. That's a good experience for kids to have. There will be plenty of other opportunities throughout their lives when they will encounter novelty. You've giving them some experiences of learning to handle novelty.

When I do presentations, I always ask who remembers which recent president of the United States hated which vegetable. Usually someone remembers it was George Bush, our 41st president (1988-1992).[15] People are always surprised and often delighted to hear that he banned broccoli from the presidential jet, Air Force One (see below for the sad story of what happened to the broccoli). I also share that he was quoted in an interview as saying "When I was a kid, my mother made me eat broccoli, and I don't have to anymore."

Photography by Gordon Werner; Graphics by
Melissa Vu – www.vu-works.com

Let me talk about this because this story is a familiar one to a lot of people. It brings up several issues about learning to like a new food, which helps us understand why requiring, forcing, or pressuring a child to eat a food is a counter-productive strategy.

1. We are not the same when it comes to tasting bitterness. Some of us have more receptor sites than average on our tongues for tasting bitterness. People with lots of receptor sites for bitterness are called "super tasters." A food, such as broccoli, will taste more bitter to these people than to most people. Apparently, one in four people are super tasters.[16]

   Of any group of foods, it is the vegetable group that has the most foods with a taste of bitterness. It is also vegetables that kids have the most trouble learning to like.

   Given the role of bitterness, I think it is helpful for parents to have some strategies for helping their child learn to like a food with some bitterness in it. The strategy used in preschools and homes of having kids dip broccoli in a salad dressing makes sense because the salad dressing helps cuts the bitterness flavor. Using sauces, cheese, and other pleasant flavorings also helps. Of course you use the strategies mentioned earlier too.

2. My experience is, if you want to make sure your child will **not like** a new food, then you should pressure or make him eat the food if he doesn't like it the first time he tries it. Making a child eat a new food that doesn't taste good to them the first time they try it, turns it into a very negative experience. Because it will also be a strong negative emotional experience, you ensure that your child will never forget this very unpleasant experience.

3. Many adults have shared with me about unpleasant experiences they had as kids during mealtimes. Some were made to stay at the table for hours until they ate all of the food on their plate. Some were made to eat a food they didn't like. The memories are strong, and they are emotional. My biggest concern is these experiences do five things:

   • They build eaters who are less capable with their eating.

   • They build eaters who have less enjoyment with eating and with mealtimes.

   • They build emotional disconnection between the parent and their child.

   • They give the child an unnecessary but quite powerful experience that he or she is powerless.

- They don't provide experiences that support their child having a genuine joy of exploring something new at a pace that is comfortable to the child.

4. Keep in mind that you may do everything right, and your child still may not like the food. I always have fun during my presentations when I ask the adults if there are specific foods they don't like. Nearly all adults will name at least one food they don't like. It is normal for an adult to have a food they like. Mine is Brussels sprouts.

There is one major strategy I haven't shared. When you get your child involved with a food, your child is more likely to want to try it. Involving your child in the food preparation and cooking are excellent ways of increasing the chances that your child will try the food. The involvement provides low-key exposure to the food and increases the child's interest and curiosity in the food being prepared.

One strategy I have used with parents is sharing a recipe and having the parents circle the steps their child could do or could help the parent do. Then the parent and the child make a shopping list for the recipe, go to the store together, and have the child be involved in picking out the food at the supermarket. Then they prepare, cook, serve, and eat the food.

Work also can be done with child care providers, early education settings, and school settings to allow children to be more involved with food. All Our Kin (http://allourkin.org) is a very innovative, savvy, and effective program in New Haven, CT that trains, supports, and sustains community child care providers to create high quality family day care programs in their homes. Not only does All Our Kin help these providers become knowledgeable about child development, they also help them learn important business skills. To be in the room with these providers is to be with a roomful of joyful entrepreneurs.

All Our Kin recently added a raised bed gardening option in which 15 providers chose to have a garden for kids on their property. All Our Kin developed a flexible garden-based curriculum with literacy-based, garden-themed experiences that could match the needs of each provider. Providers also received weekly educational consultant visits. An evaluation report will be released later this year, but providers are already reporting that kids are eating more vegetables at snack time and requesting vegetables more often. Kids became involved with the food preparation. One of the educators connected with the program would periodically prepare a snack for the kids made with vegetables from the garden while in the garden. They report the kids love having the garden. The kids help plant and care for the plants. Some sites even have dig beds where the kids were free to dig in the dirt. All Our Kin hopes to expand this project next year to an additional 30 providers.

Dr. Isobel Contento did some research with 600 children designed to get them to eat more vegetables and whole grains. As reported in the New York Times, the kids who received the lessons on healthy eating and had experiences cooking were more likely to eat the foods they cooked than the children who didn't receive the cooking experiences.[17] In fact, they were more likely to ask for additional servings.

Keep in mind that one big purpose of having your child help with the food selection, preparation, and cooking is to provide a time of emotional connection between you and your child. Mothers who do this tell me it really is a time of emotional connection. That is a huge gift to you and to your child.

By the way, if you're looking for an excellent resource on shopping at the supermarket with your young child, you should check out pages 15-20 of "Grocery Shopping with Families" at http://www.cdph.ca.gov/programs/wicworks/Documents/NE/WIC-NE-LessonPlans-Other-Shopping-GroceryShoppingWithFamilies English.doc

I wanted to share one last story with you. One mom shared how she loved fresh asparagus in the springtime, but her young daughter wasn't interested. One day the mom was standing by sink washing fresh asparagus spears. She was also eating a few of them and enjoying the flavor. Her daughter was next to her, watching her, and noticing how much her mother was enjoying the asparagus. She finally asked her mom for a stalk. The mom told me her daughter took a bite of the asparagus, chewed it, and made the face that kids make when tasting something they've never tasted before. Then her daughter told her she liked it.

I share this story because a parent's reaction to a new food has a strong influence on their child. Your willingness to be adventurous about trying a new food also has an influence on your child. The comments you make about a food also has an influence on your child.

I hope this has been helpful for you and has shown you that offering new foods to a child is another way to give your genuine love, care, and connection and to support your child's healthy development.

Food for Thought

1. Parents often communicate a strong reaction when their child likes or dislikes a food. What can you do in order to stay neutral?

2. If you give your child a challenge by offering a new food but do so without loving support, what sort of experience does your child have? Would your child have a different experience with the challenge if he also received your loving support?

3. What is your response to the statement "providing a challenge and also giving your loving support is being a powerful parent?"

4. Identify two steps you will use to help your child learn to like a new food.

CHAPTER 8:

Learning about Different Levels of Hunger and Fullness

One dad shared with me how his kids weren't eating well at dinner. This bothered him, but he didn't want to make dinner a time of stress by pressuring his kids to eat. Instead, he began taking them out to run around and play for 30 minutes before dinner. That resulted in his kids having a better appetite and mealtime becoming more pleasant.

I liked what this father did because he came up with a creative solution. He acted in a savvy manner because he took an action that helped increase the odds that his children would come to dinner with a good appetite.

A savvy parent will build a mealtime environment that increases the likelihood their child will come to a meal with a good appetite. The child's appetite is a force that can be your ally, and you can use it to help build your child's eating capabilities and life skills. So, let's talk about appetite some more.

Have you ever had your child come to a meal and surprise you by the size of her appetite?

Have you ever had a meal when your child had little or no appetite?

Can you look at your child and know if her appetite is big, small, or in between?

What we know is that it is normal for kids' appetite to vary. Sometimes they have a huge appetite. Sometimes they have a small or no appetite. Often their appetite falls in between.

When I do presentations with preschool teachers and parents, I ask them if I can look at them and know who is hungry, who is full, and who is in between. Of course, they tell me I can't. Which is true. I tell them they are the expert and the only expert about how hungry or full they feel. Then I tell them that this is also true about their kids. Their kids are the expert and the only expert about how hungry or full they feel.

Then we talk about why a child might have a large appetite and why a child might have a small or no appetite.

A child may have a large appetite if:

- She is going through a growth spurt.

- She has been quite active.

- She is getting over an illness and her appetite is returning.

On the other hand, her appetite could be small because

- She just finished a growth spurt.

- She hasn't had much physical activity.

- She is starting an illness.

- She may have an underlying problem that makes it painful to eat.

When it comes to your child's appetite, you have four jobs:

1. Help your child have her appetite.

2. Accept your child's appetite as it is (large, moderate, small, or no appetite).

3. Help your child practice paying attention to her level of hunger and fullness.

4. Support your child being in charge of how much or how little she eats.

1. Help your child have an appetite

The action you take will be designed to help your child be most likely to come to a meal or snack with a good appetite. That is your job. You will use two strategies. One strategy is to prevent the loss of your child's appetite. The other strategy is to increase the chances that your child will have a good appetite.

The first strategy is preventing your child from losing their appetite before a scheduled meal or snack. You don't allow your child to eat before a meal or snack. You have her wait until the meal or snack time to eat. Thus, you are using your power to help your child have an appetite by not letting your child snack anytime she wants. By having your child wait until the scheduled time for the snack or meal, you are making it likely that your child come to the meal or snack with a good appetite.

The other key strategy is to create a mealtime environment that helps ensure your child will likely come to the meal or snack with an appetite. Basically, it is giving your child an opportunity to be physically active before a meal or snack so your child is likely to have a good appetite.

Preventing your child's appetite loss and helping your child to have a good appetite accomplish two things. It makes mealtime more pleasant because your child is focused on eating. Also, a child with a good appetite is more likely to try a new food.

Some schools are using a similar strategy as this dad. Several years ago I spoke David Schwake with the Litchfield School District in Litchfield Park, Arizona about their strategy of switching recess to be before lunch rather than after lunch. David commented "*although there were no studies done, I can assure you that the teachers would revolt if we decided to go back. Kids get a chance to cool/calm down while eating, plate waste is reduced, and teachers pick up at least 5-7 minutes per day in teaching time as students are ready to start learning as soon as they come to class from lunch.*

I also spoke with Denise Higgins at the Douglas County School District in Nevada. She shared how one elementary school in the district had switched recess to be before lunch rather than after lunch. Denise shared, "*We have a morning nutrition break for this school because they eat a little later than they would have if recess were not first. This nutrition break is wildly successful for both the kids and our program. Our monthly revenue is approximately $1,500 from this break alone. We do not sell snacks at this school (we do at other elementary schools) during lunchtime. I have not done a formal study but by observance I have found the following:*

- *Kids eat more as they are not in a hurry to go outside and play plus they are hungrier. They sit there until the bell rings to go to class.*

- *They drink more milk and purchase more water - I guess they are thirstier.*

- *They are calmer during the lunchtime. I guess this is because they got all the "play" out of them during the recess portion of the break*

Both schools have done a good job of helping their students have a good appetite.

By the way, one of my pet peeves is that elementary schools are missing a huge opportunity to support their students social, emotional, physical, cognitive, and language development by not having adults sit with the students, by not focusing on building a mealtime environment that supports their students healthy development, and by not using the mealtime as part of the day's learning environment. When kids go from preschool to kindergarten and later grades they are given larger challenges in regard to their learning. Yet, in nearly all elementary schools, they are often given less support and fewer challenges about their eating capability than when they were in preschool.

In fact, adults are often put into policing roles in the cafeteria, hurrying the kids to eat, telling them where to eat, not to socialize with friends and telling kids what they have dropped or made a mess. Kids may be punished and made to sweep the floor or clean the tables, all reinforcing the behavior of eating quickly, mindlessly and without talking with friends.

If an elementary school's principal, teachers, cafeteria manager, and parents are interested in a wonderful approach that integrates simple cooking and tasting of a variety of foods, I recommend you take a serious look at Antonia Demas' curriculum, Food Is Elementary. Antonia has worked with hundreds of elementary schools to implement this curriculum. Kids prepare recipes from around the world, which helps them appreciate other cultures. Antonia's website can be accessed at www.foodstudies.org.

Ariel Demas, who uses the Food Is Elementary curriculum in Baltimore, states on her school's website, "The universal nature of food makes it easy to incorporate many disciplines, including botany, geography, history, chemistry, math, art, and music." Students at her school end up preparing and trying 12 different beans from around the world, a large variety of greens, and a large variety of whole grains. They actually eat them, and they enjoy them. In some schools the cafeteria has started to offer the same foods.

If you want to see a school that has seized the opportunity to use food to create an enjoyable, joyful, developmentally savvy, and safe learning experience, check out Ariel's webpage at Hampstead Hill Academy in Baltimore - http://www.hha47.org/academics/ffl.

When I first called Hampstead Hill Academy in Baltimore, I spoke with Christine Kotchenreuthar in the school office and told her why I wanted to talk with Ariel Demas about the Food Is Elementary program. She told me that kids are now asking to have more garlic and onions added to the food. She also had me laughing as she told me she was initially quite skeptical about this whole approach. She in fact told the principal that the addition of this curriculum would cause kids to riot. But that is not what happened. Kids love preparing and tasting the foods. The school's food educator, Ariel Demas, uses the "No yuck" rule to help kids learn to maintain a pleasant mealtime environment. Kids are encouraged but not required or pressured to try the food they have prepared. Ariel shared with me that one child went for months before deciding to taste one of the foods he and other students prepared. Ariel's respectful way of teaching provides challenges to the students in the form of new foods but allows them to go at a pace that fits the uniqueness of each student. At its core Ariel's approach is building trust and a joy of learning. Those are huge gifts.

It actually gets even better. The school goes from pre-K through the 8th grade. All of the students attend the Food for Life class for 45 minutes every two weeks. The older students help prepare healthy and tasty snacks for teachers' meetings and school events. Some of the other things you will find at Hampstead Hill Academy, as described on their website, are:

- Culinary Arts Club - this is an after school program on Fridays. Not only do the students focus on learning special cooking techniques and learning from local guest chefs, they prepare the food for and host monthly community dinners.

- <u>Community Dinners</u> – the students prepare delicious, nutritious, theme-based meals made from scratch. Community Dinners are fun for the whole family, offering inexpensive, fresh food complimented by live performances by the HHA chorus, band and orchestra.

- <u>Healthy Snacks at School Events</u> – students also prepare delicious and nutritious snacks at all school events and staff meetings. Teachers love having these wonderful snacks, and this has increased teachers' exposure to a variety of foods that were unfamiliar to them.

- <u>Garden Club</u> – The students maintain the school garden. They have "different beds representing foods that are native to different continents." The garden also contains a wide variety of plants that are native to Maryland, a butterfly garden, and a "sense-sational garden" to please the 5 senses.

The Food is Elementary curriculum allows a school to start setting its own agenda of using food to support children's learning and development. A core requirement is having the principal on board with this program and supporting it. Matthew Hornbeck, the principal at Hampstead Hill School loves this program and actively supports it. One other school in Baltimore, Stadium School, has a full-time food educator and four other schools have part-time food educators one day per week. Matthew loves this program so much he had another classroom built at Hampstead Hill School that is designed as a kitchen classroom.

<u>2. Accept your child's appetite as it is (large, moderate, small, or no appetite)</u>

One of the huge gifts you can give your child is your acceptance, particularly acceptance of their uniqueness. Accepting a child as she genuinely is provides wonderful support for your child. As I discussed earlier, it is normal for a child's appetite to vary. Your child's appetite will not be the same every time.

An important strategy a parent can use is to help their child become aware of their different levels of hunger and fullness. I cover this more in the next section. Basically, your job is to let your child be in charge of her appetite level and accepting what she says about the level of her appetite. You then end up letting her appetite level be her business, not your business. You provide wonderful support when you help your child practice paying attention to her level of hunger/fullness and eating accordingly.

Keep in mind, as you accept your child's appetite as it is, you still want to focus on feeding your love, care, and connection.

3. Help your child practice paying attention to her level of hunger and fullness

Dr. Susan Johnson did some amazing research that was published by the Journal of Pediatrics in December 2000.[18]

She and her team designed a simple approach to help preschoolers become aware of their different levels of hunger and fullness. Next, they worked with the preschoolers during their mid-morning snack time to pay attention to the feelings of hunger and fullness in their stomachs. They helped each child learn to pay attention to whether their stomach was telling them they were hungry, a little full, or very full. During their normal mid-morning snack time, all children were prompted at least 2 times to check in and see if they were still hungry and whether they wanted to eat more. Basically, they were teaching each child to be aware of their internal cues of hunger and satiety and creating a mealtime environment that supported the children using that awareness to decide how much to eat. What was so amazing was that preschoolers who had been over-eating stopped overeating; preschoolers who had been under-eating ate more.

To my knowledge this is the only research that has demonstrated you could restore young children's capability to self-regulate – that is, to pay attention to their own hunger and fullness levels and eat as a much or as little as they needed and then stop eating.

Helping your child acquire the ability to self-regulate with their eating is providing your child with a very important life skill. The Nobel Prize winning economist, Dr. James Heckman, has analyzed the impact of high quality child care programs with longitudinal data into the children's early adult years.[19] [20] Interestingly, he points out that the source of the high quality child care programs' impact is the building of what he calls "soft skills" or "character skills." "Character skills" are such capabilities as being able to control yourself, perseverance, attentiveness and sociability. Also, if you haven't read How Children Succeed by Paul Tough, I highly recommend it. He makes a wonderful case for helping children achieve non-cognitive skills such as the "character skills" covered by Heckman, in addition to the strong focus put on cognitive skills. In essence, "character skills" and "non-cognitive skills" are personal and inter-personal capacities needed to thrive in life. A key point is these skills are built within relationships, particularly quality relationships that have the quality of interactions found in the pattern of caregiving that builds secure attachment.

This is a strategy you can use to build your child's eating capability. You help your child learn about her different levels of hunger and fullness that her stomach is telling her. Then you gently ask her at the beginning, middle, and towards the end of a meal what her stomach is telling her.

You can also share what your stomach is telling you. This focus on awareness of hunger and fullness levels can be done in low key and even fun way and can become a natural part of the mealtime routine. In today's eating environment, kids, more than ever, need this capability.

<u>4. Support your child being in charge of how much or how little she eats</u>

One of the things that make life easier and better is having someone on our side. Kids especially need an adult on their side. Just having one adult on their side makes a huge difference for a kid.

When you let your child be in charge of how much (or how little) she eats, you are providing powerful support. Basically, you are letting her eating be her business, not your business. Thus, you are giving your child your blessing that she can be in charge of how much (or how little) she eats, and you will not try to take over her job. Your support allows her to handle the different levels of hunger and fullness she will have, which supports her in becoming more capable with her eating.

Part of your support is helping your child be aware of her different levels of hunger and fullness and providing several opportunities during the meal for her to check in to find out what her stomach is telling her about her level of hunger or fullness. Then, if your child only wants to eat a little that is fine with you. Or if your child wants seconds, that is fine with you.

The Gifts for Your Child

You provide several gifts to your child by providing these developmentally healthy experiences.

- Your child learns that she can have and survive her feelings of hunger.

- She learns she can then experience getting enough to eat at the next meal or snack to take away her feelings of hunger.

- Your child gets to learn that if she chooses not to eat at a meal or snack that she may have strong feelings of hunger in 30-90 minutes. This builds an understanding of natural consequences: if I do this (not eat at a meal or snack), then this will happen (I will have feelings of hunger). As she sees that you will indeed stick to this schedule of having a meal or snack every 2-3 hours, she will learn she may want to go ahead and eat some to tide herself over until the next meal or snack.

The Gifts for You

Just as importantly, you provide several gifts to yourself by providing these developmentally healthy experiences.

- When you provide a mealtime environment that allows your child to experience her feelings of hunger and fullness, and you provide enough food so your child can get enough to eat to no longer feel hungry, you are doing powerful and loving parenting.

  Let me say this again because it is important. When you provide a mealtime environment that allows your child to experience her feelings of hunger and fullness, and you provide enough food at the meal or snack so your child can get enough to eat and no longer feel hungry, you are doing powerful and loving parenting.

- The truth is a parent cannot look at their child and know how hungry she is. Your child is the best person for knowing how hungry she is. You get the gift of knowing that you are building your child's capability to trust what her body is telling her. You are helping her to internalize the act of self awareness and self care. I think in today's culture girls and boys receive very little support for developing their capability to check-in with themselves to determine their own hunger/fullness level and to eat accordingly. I think our children need to learn to trust and not fear what their body is telling them about their hunger and fullness. Teaching your child to do that and supporting them to do that is an act of love by you and helps your child to learn to love herself.

- You provide the developmentally supportive structure that allows your child to have a challenge. If you allowed her to eat whenever she wanted, she would not have a challenge. Children learn and grow from the challenges they face. Challenges are opportunities for them to build their capability, learn effective strategies, experience loving support, learn natural consequences to decisions made, gain positive emotional connection, and build resiliency.

- You allow your child to have an experience that allows her to be aware of her genuine feelings of hunger. This is developmentally healthy learning.

- You allow your child to have an experience that allows her to learn she can survive the feelings of hunger and then experience getting enough to eat to take away the feelings of hunger. It is strong and loving parenting to give your child a developmentally appropriate challenge. Waiting 2-3 hours to eat again is developmentally appropriate. Having to wait 4, 5, or more hours to eat again is not developmentally appropriate.

As you do this time after time after time, you are helping provide a pattern of a developmentally healthy experience. This pattern of experience will allow your child to learn by experience she can survive these feelings of hunger, and she can develop trust she will always get enough to eat. Thus you are building her capacity to live with some feelings of hunger and you are building her level of genuine trust she will get enough to eat at each meal or snack. These are great gifts.

Food for Thought

1. How can a parent use their child's appetite as an ally?

2. What is your response to the statement that a child is the expert and the only expert about how hungry or full they feel?

3. What are 2 actions you can take to support your child's awareness of their own level of hunger and fullness?

CHAPTER 9:

Learning to Experience a Pattern of Trust

© Phyllis Meredith – www.phyllismeredith.com

Have you ever been with someone you knew in your heart deeply and consistently cared for you? Someone you feel safe around, and who doesn't force you to do something? Someone who genuinely listens to you? Someone who is genuinely on your side? That is a person you can genuinely trust.

Perhaps you have someone like that in your life. Maybe not.

Having trust is a wonderful gift. Having trust makes life richer, more enjoyable, and more emotionally safe and secure.

A child's trust is built by the love, care, and connection given by the child's parents and other important people in the child's life. The interactions that take place between parent and child are where trust is built, damaged, or an opportunity to build trust is missed.

Perfect Parenting vs. Good Enough Parenting
Perfect parenting tries to make every interaction a trust building interaction. Trying to be a perfect parent will cause you to not have peace in your life and will result in a lot of judgment by you against yourself. Not good.

So let's focus on good enough parenting so you win and your child wins. The truth is both of you are very important.

Trust vs. Mistrust
Mealtimes are an important place where trust can be built. As you incorporate developmentally healthy mealtime strategies, you are using behaviors that build your child's trust.

Having a mealtime that is pleasant and enjoyable with the parent being at the meal with the child builds trust. Allowing the child to learn to like a new food at their own pace and without being pressured to eat the new food builds trust. Providing meals and snacks on a regular and predictable schedule and allowing your child to be in charge of how much or how little he eats builds trust. Building a meal that has some foods that your child usually likes and some foods he is learning to like builds trust. Including your child in conversations at a meal or snack and genuinely listening to what he has to say builds trust. Helping your child learn manners and learn to listen when others talk builds trust. Finding out about your child's day and encouraging your child to share more about something that happened during their day builds trust. Including your child in preparing some of the food and having it be a time of connection builds trust. Having fun or silly moments and genuine laughter during meals and snacks builds trust. Offering a new food to your child and allowing your child to use his power by deciding whether or not to eat it builds trust.

As you can imagine, doing the opposite will not build trust; it will build distrust. Distrust in you and distrust in the world, but, mostly, distrust in himself. Rather than focusing on connecting with others, exploring the world, and genuinely enjoying life, the child's focus instead becomes about protecting himself. Energy your child could be using to explore, learn, connect, and live is spent, instead, on protecting himself.

When you use these healthy mealtime strategies consistently, you are providing a pattern of trust building. A pattern of experience provided to an infant or child results in the creation of an internal belief in the infant/child. For example, an infant who has a pattern of experience of being fed whenever he gives a cue he is hungry will develop internal trust that his hunger signals will be consistently noticed and will quickly lead to him being fed. Suppose this happens 8-10 times a day for 180 days in a row with an infant. Another way to look at it is to see that this infant would have this positive experience 1400-1800 times in six months. A pattern this strong would lead to a high level of trust. I believe this type of care is more likely to result in a child who has an internal and genuine belief that he is loved. That is powerful parenting.

What we know from early childhood development research and brain development research is that one key way to develop a belief in a child (ex. I can trust people close to me) is to provide a type of care over and over so that it becomes a pattern of care.

So, let's look at mealtimes with children. What are some of the things your child will learn when you use a pattern of developmentally healthy mealtime strategies? These are some I can think of:

- I can trust that mealtime will be a pleasant time.

- I can trust that I will be given love, care, and connection at mealtimes.

- I can trust I will be noticed, accepted, and cherished at mealtimes.

- I can trust that I will be listened to at mealtimes.

- I can trust I will be allowed to go at my own pace about learning to like new foods.

- I can trust that others will be given an opportunity to share at mealtimes.

- I can trust I will have emotional safety during a meal or snack.

Why is this trust so important?

Developmentally, a child who has a high level of trust has a lower stress level and has a greater desire to explore. I bring this up because a genuine desire to explore and a joy of exploring are so important to developing a genuine joy of learning. I believe a child who has a genuine joy of learning is more likely to be successful in life.

There is some fascinating and quite important research that has looked at why some kids have more trust and explore more than other kids.[21] Some of the research has also followed these kids for 20 years or more. This research is about attachment.

Basically, attachment research says the quality and the pattern of care in the relationship between a parent who cares for a young child and the child is "central to a child's later functioning in life."[22] The quality of the care and the quality of the interactions between a parent and young child make a huge difference to the child. I think it also makes huge difference to the parent.

A young child's pattern of experience of receiving good enough parenting creates an internal expectation in the child. For example, good enough parenting can create the expectation in your child that he can trust that he will be treated with warmth and care. It can also create an expectation in your child that he can trust he will be treated with warmth and care in close relationships with others. That is one of the profound lessons your child is learning about life – how he can expect to be treated in his close relationships in life.

However, a child can also have a pattern of care that does not build trust. The main reason I bring this up is because there is a potential and important gift to the parent for exploring why the parent has trouble using behaviors that build trust in their child.

My experience is every parent, including myself, has been wounded by experiences within their families during their own childhood. Our wounds are sometimes very clear to us and sometimes hidden. Some of the wounds have left scars, strong memories, and a lasting impact on us. Other wounds have taken an incredible toll on us. Some of us are lucky to be alive. Some of us run from our wounds, some of us deny our wounds, and some of us are even unaware of them. And we know that some did not make it out of childhood alive.

I emphasize the issue of woundedness because our wounds have built distrust in us, especially the wounds from powerful, negative experiences and the wounds that came from a pattern of care. A parent's distrust from their own childhood can play a powerful role in the quality of interactions provided by a parent today.

A struggle in your relationship with your young child can be an opportunity for a parent to gain awareness about their own woundedness.

I bring this up because some of the struggles a parent has with their relationship with their child will occur at mealtimes.

So, as you start to incorporate developmentally healthy mealtime behaviors, you may start to have a greater awareness of the struggles you are having at mealtimes with your child or you may encounter some new struggles. It may be difficult to use a particular mealtime strategy, it may be emotionally draining to use a strategy, or you may even encounter anger or rage about using one of the mealtime strategies. You can fight it, deny it, or push it away, but that doesn't resolve it. My experience is the only way to deal with a struggle is to accept that it is present, start to explore it, and don't blame your child.

Basically, your struggle with your child's eating can indicate:

- You need some additional tools, such as healthy mealtime strategies and understanding about children's eating.

- You may have some woundedness from your own childhood that is interfering with you being able to feed your love, care, and connection to your child.

- You may have some woundedness from your own childhood that is interfering with your child being able to receive your love, care, and connection.

- You need some additional tools, and you have some woundedness from your own childhood that needs to be addressed.

One of the risks with a struggle you are having with your child at mealtimes is that you can put the blame for the struggle on the child. You think it is caused 100% by the child. You believe your child is completely to blame. So, if you think and believe that your child is the complete cause of this struggle, then the solution becomes – make my child change and do exactly what I want. Then you and your child have a battle. Or else your child complies but doesn't gain important life skills and eating capabilities.

The reason I'm focusing on the issue of struggles at mealtimes is because each struggle is an opportunity for a parent to use the struggle as a starting point to make changes, sometimes difficult changes, which will build more trust in your child and more peace and less stress in the parent.

The trick is to first stop yourself from blaming your child for the struggle and focusing on yourself instead. This can be hard emotional work, especially when you hit the spot of not blaming your child but not yet having a solution to the struggle. That is a difficult place to be, but, with help, you can move through it and out of it.

A key part of a parent's work is first just becoming aware of the struggle and then accepting the truth that you are having a struggle. Let me say that from my own experience that there is always a huge gift for you on the other side of the struggle. The gift is connected with having more peace, being able to receive more love, and/or being able to freely offer more love. But, the awareness and acceptance must come first.

When you can help create a family in which genuine love, care and connection can be given easier and more freely and the love, care and connection is more likely to be received, you are doing powerful parenting.

Woundedness and Beliefs about Love

The other major reason I bring up the issue of woundedness is that the experiences and the patterns of experiences that caused our woundedness also left us with beliefs about love. Our experiences and patterns of experience with the care we received as infants, toddlers, and young children taught some of us that love is warm, accepting, dependable, soothing, consistent, and comforting. It may have taught us that we can trust in our hearts that we are genuinely loved. This kind of care and patterns of care build an internal belief in the child that their needs are important and their needs are ok to have. It may have taught us that our mere existence brings joy and delight to others. Kids who receive this kind of care trust they will receive help about their needs and the help will be good.

However, some of us have had experiences and patterns of experience with the care we received as infants, toddlers, and young children that may have taught us that love is inconsistent, cold, or unavailable. This kind of care and patterns of care build an internal belief in the child that their needs may or may not be important and their needs may or may not be ok to have. Kids who receive this kind of care do not trust they will consistently and predictably receive help about their needs and the help will be good. Rather than coming to trust that their needs are good, they may start to believe that their needs are shameful or even unsafe and should be hidden rather than communicated.

For others, our experiences and patterns of experience with the care we received as infants, toddlers, and young children taught us that love is actually frightening, hurtful, or even terrifying. This likely taught us that we can trust in our hearts that we are loved, but it is a love that means pain, fear, terror, and/or rejection. Kids who receive this kind of care do not trust they will receive help about their needs nor believe the help will be good. Rather than coming to trust that their needs are good, they may start to believe their needs will cause pain, fear, terror, or rejection.

The person(s) they need to be their source of protection and care is their source of fear, pain, terror, and rejection. Rather than learning other people can be a source of comfort and help, the child learns important people in your life are a source of fear, pain, and terror. Rather than developing a positive emotional connection with someone close and important to the child, the child develops emotional disconnection. Rather than learning to signal and to ask for help and receive reassurance, the child learns it is safer and better to depend on himself or learns that it is safer and better to retreat and not depend on others.

These beliefs formed in a child from their own early experiences and patterns of experience are powerful beliefs. A big part of what makes them so powerful is that they are at work, especially in regard to relationships with others, in three strong and foundational ways:

- <u>Foundational Perspective</u> – these early experiences and patterns of experience create a foundational perspective in the child about how the child views his needs and about how the child views his parents and other important caregivers. This becomes the basis for the child's perspective about life. Thus, she may view life as good, unpredictable, uncaring, or hurtful.

- <u>Foundational Expectations</u> - these early experiences and patterns of experience create foundational expectations in a child about the care they can expect to receive and expectations about the world. Thus, for example, the child will end up with an expectation that the world is generally safe, is inconsistently safe, is unsafe, or is terrifying.

- <u>Foundational Gate-keeper</u> –imagine a gatekeeper stationed at the entrance to a castle. When someone comes to a gate at a castle, the gate-keeper decides if this person is a threat or is an ally. Early experiences and patterns of experience basically build a gate in the child's mind that interprets, or misinterprets, the actions of others. The early experiences and patterns of experience that were genuinely loving and built trust and connection will build a strong gate-keeper that does a good job of interpreting if another person is safe or if the person is likely not safe. The early experiences and patterns of experience that were frightening, hurtful, or even terrifying will build a weak gate-keeper or no gate-keeper at all and allows anyone who shows up at the gate to come in. The early experiences and patterns of experience that were inconsistent, cold, or unavailable will build a gate-keeper that is confused and unsure about the people who show up at the gate.

Please hear that I am not sharing any of this to condemn any parent or to make a parent feel guilty. I truly want parents to know they are genuinely powerful and important people in their child's life. I believe a parent is powerful and important in their child's life by their presence, by their absence, by what a parent does, and by what a parent does not do. In other words, once you are a child's parent, it is a given that you will have a powerful impact on your child. My desire is each parent will grow to become an even more powerful and life-giving influence on their child's healthy development.

What is true is a child needs their parent, particularly the parent's love, care, and connection. A child needs a parent on their side in a way that is supportive and yet in a way that allows their child to face and then successfully handle developmentally appropriate challenges.

What is also true is that each parent is called to be aware of their own parenting behaviors with their child and to try to understand if their behaviors are building trust or building distrust. When a parent takes the time and has the courage to look at their parenting behaviors that is a huge gift of love to your child. The next big step is accepting the parenting behaviors that are building trust and accepting the parenting behaviors that may not be building trust. This is another huge gift of love to your child. Taking the steps of awareness and acceptance allows you to take ownership.

Taking ownership may result in some healthy guilt or some healthy shame. This is completely normal. The trick is to not let your guilt or shame stop you from taking action to get help about learning some new parenting behaviors. Many of the mealtime behaviors I've discussed in previous chapters can be viewed as new parenting behaviors that help build trust in your child, help build emotional connection between you and your child, and help build important capabilities and life skills in your child.

Also, keep in mind that your acts of awareness, acceptance, and learning some new parenting behaviors are deep acts of forgiveness on your part. In a sense it is sacrificial love because you have given up an old way of parenting and adopted a new parenting behavior. Thus, you have voluntarily and willingly given up a part of yourself. That is a deep, deep act of love.

If you want to learn more about how these beliefs are formed and why they are so powerful, I highly recommend <u>A General Theory of Love</u> by Thomas Lewis, Fari Amani, and Richard Lannon.[23] It is the best book I have read that helped me understand the power of a parent's healthy or unhealthy love. It helped me understand why a parent's love, care, and connection are so powerful. I particularly recommend chapters 2, 4, and 7.

Food for Thought

1. Why does having trust make life richer or more enjoyable for your child?

2. Why would children with high levels of trust have lower stress levels?

3. How do wounds from a parent's childhood affect their own parenting beliefs?

4. Can you think of a time when you used a struggle you were having with your child to gain awareness about yourself and make a change in your parenting?

CHAPTER 10:

Learning to Experience a Pattern of Warmth, Acceptance, Interest, Delight, and Having Someone on Your Side

Mavis Bomengen was working with a mother to help her two-year-old son, who was enrolled in the nationwide Special Supplemental Nutrition Program for Women, Infants, and Children (WIC). As part of the WIC visit, Mavis explored the child's mealtime environment and learned that the child to was having to "clean his plate" at each meal.

The tension and battles that resulted made mealtimes unpleasant for both the child and his mother. Mavis offered the mother another mealtime strategy: the division of responsibility.[24] The mother was willing to try to incorporate this concept by letting the child-- and not either parent--assume responsibility for how much he ate. However, the mother warned that the response of the child's father would probably be a different story. It turns out the father was insisting his son eat all of the food on his plate. Mavis realized she needed to reach the father in order for the family mealtime environment to change. After three calls to the father, he agreed to meet Mavis in the clinic to discuss the situation.

Mavis asked him about his own experience of mealtime when he was a child. The answer was not surprising: He had been forced to clean his plate. "If it was good enough for me," he stated, "it's good enough for my son." And how had he felt about mealtimes under those circumstances? Mavis asked. Mealtimes were unpleasant, the father admitted. Then, faced with the realization that his son was probably having similar feelings, the father agreed to let his son decide how much to eat at each meal.[25]

Have you ever had someone who lights up when they see you, who shows their genuine warmth and delight to see you, accepts you as you are, and gives you a sense of being on your side?

Many of us have. It feels wonderful. It makes life richer and so much easier and better. I had two uncles like that.

However, like the father in this story and his son, many of us haven't. It is a huge loss to not have someone like that in our lives. My mom and dad could not say "I love you" or give any physical affection when I was a child. As a child I thought that was normal. As an adult, I realized I missed out on some very important experiences. That lack of love created some woundedness in me. I realized this left me with a deep hunger for love and without good skills for finding this love and receiving it in a healthy relationship. But, I also learned with the help of healthy people it is possible as an adult to receive this kind of love. I also learned being able to receive this kind of love makes life richer, more enjoyable, and less stressful.

I bring this up because mealtimes can be powerful opportunities for your child to receive your warmth, acceptance, interest, delight, and having someone stronger on their side. These are not small gifts to a child. They help your child develop into a secure, loved, and loving person. They truly are important and life-giving gifts. And clearly, our world needs more adults who are secure, loved, and loving. That is why this father at the beginning of the chapter is doing such powerful work.

So, what is the opposite of each? I would say the opposite of warmth is indifference; the opposite of acceptance is rejection; the opposite of interest is being ignored; the opposite of delight is hostility; and the opposite of having someone on your side is having someone who ignores you or someone who attacks you verbally, emotionally, and/or physically.

Every time I have given a presentation about building healthy mealtime environments and ask the adults in the audience if anyone, during their childhood, had been made to either eat all of the food on their plate or made to eat a food they didn't like, there are always several adults who reveal that this happened to them. I'm aware there likely are other adults in each audience who also experienced this but, as an act of love, choose not to reveal that information.

For the child, the experience of being made to eat all of the food on her plate by a parent when her appetite is telling her she isn't very hungry is an experience of not having the parent on her side. In a sense, the child has lost the loving protection of her parent. I would say the child has also lost her parent's acceptance. Obviously, the child is not experiencing her parent's genuine warmth or delight.

The same thing is true when a child is made to eat a food the child hasn't yet learned to like. It provides an emotional experience of not having the parent on her side. It provides an emotional experience of not being offered her parent's warmth, acceptance, and delight.

When a parent uses healthy mealtime behaviors, the parent creates a mealtime environment in which the parent can offer their genuine warmth, acceptance, interest, and delight and offer their child the experience of having her parent on her side. These are huge gifts to your child, and this type of parenting is powerful parenting.

I think children who are routinely offered their parent's authentic warmth, acceptance, and delight, and who genuinely experience having their parent on their side grow up to be more secure in themselves, grow up to like themselves better, and grow up to be a more capable and pleasant person. I think they grow up finding it easier to receive love and to give love, which are foundational gifts for making life richer both in present time and in the years to come.

102

I think parents who are able to create this type of healthy mealtime environment have a greater level of satisfaction about their parenting and a greater sense they are parenting in a way that helps their child be more likely to be successful in life. These are pretty good feelings to have.

If you find you are stuck in a pattern of not being able to offer your child your genuine warmth, acceptance, interest, delight, and/or experience of having you on her side, just use it as a sign that something is present in you that is getting in the way of doing so. Perhaps you don't know how to show your delight or interest because no one ever did that with you. Maybe mealtimes were so wounding for you as a child, and for no fault of your own, it is difficult to offer your acceptance, warmth, and interest at a mealtime. Perhaps this is true for your spouse but not for you, and your spouse doesn't want to even begin to look at this stuff from their past.

This kind of struggle with parenting is something I believe most parents encounter. It is the struggle of giving your child something you didn't receive as a child. Not only is there an internal sense of incompetence because we may not feel like we're any good at it, but there is also the feeling of having our old childhood experiences awakened or felt at a deeper level. I think this is truly some of the most challenging and difficult work of growing as a parent. Rather than avoiding it, we are called to welcome it into our presence, reexamine it, discuss it, and think about the conclusions we drew about ourselves as kids from these experiences. There is also the rest of the healing work that needs to happen.

There will likely be a need to get help in learning how to parent to offer more of your warmth, acceptance, interest, delight, and/or your child experiencing having you on their side. You may feel weak or scared about getting help. You may feel ashamed of needing help. You may feel guilt as you become aware of the limitations of your parenting. Don't let this stop you. Taking action to improve your parenting is an incredible act of love. It is an act of love to your child and to yourself.

In situations like these, the Circle of Security Parenting© (COS P) concept of "Shark Music" is particularly valuable. "Shark Music" is a term used to describe a situation in which a parent interprets a need their child is having (ex. a need to explore; a need to be comforted) that is actually a safe need, but the parent interprets the child's need as unsafe and reacts negatively to their child. Seeing how "Shark Music" works while watching the COS P DVD is actually quite powerful.

The phrase "Shark Music" gives non-shaming language to a parent to use to describe their own internal reaction to a need their child is having. Using the phrase "Shark Music" allows the parent to achieve a shift from blaming the child to understanding it is their own struggle that is taking place. Basically, use of "Shark Music" gives a parent the gift of awareness and allows the parent to use their power to take ownership of their reaction rather than blaming their child. The beauty of "Shark Music" is it allows a parent to have and provide more genuine empathy to their child. It is interesting to see so many parents be able to adopt and use "Shark Music" and then see the positive improvement in the relationship with their child.

You may encounter a big lie during this process. The big lie says it is too late to do this work to make a difference to your child. While your child may have had some wounding, your child can still benefit and benefit mightily by you growing and being able to offer more of your genuine warmth, acceptance, interest, delight, and experience of having you on their side.

Again, COS P is by far the best parenting curriculum I've come across that genuinely helps parents achieve a significant, positive, and lasting change in their relationship with their children. Part of the beauty of COS P is the underlying principle that it is never too late for a parent to restore their relationship with their child.

Keep in mind that every other parent is imperfect too. You may look at another parent and think they have it together, but that is a lie.

By the way, my favorite parents are those parents who can see their flaws and shortcomings, accept them, and take action to make some improvements. These parents have a wonderful spirit about them. These parents also have more and more genuine life in them each year. They aren't perfect, but they're on a path of growing, and that makes such a difference.

As a parent, if you are encountering regret about the mealtime en-vironment you may have created in the past, be sure to give yourself credit for your awareness and sensitivity. Those are important traits for growing more genuine love in your family.

What is true is some parents are not aware or sensitive about the unpleasant experiences their children have had at mealtimes due to the mealtime environment the parent helped to create. Some adults have shared with me about experiencing a rigid mealtime environ-ment in which there wasn't much warmth, delight, and acceptance, and they were made to eat all of the food on their plate. When I've reflected this must have been unpleasant for them and for their parents, some will agree with me, but some have shared that they perceived their parents as unaware of their children's unpleasant experiences.

Some share that they perceived their parents as enjoying the rigid mealtime environment. That is a tough situation for a child because there isn't much empathy about the child's experiences at mealtimes. That can be quite wounding to the child. I find a parent is usually like this because of their own experience growing up, but they have never examined it. As a result, they miss out on life-changing growth that results in them having more genuine love and their kids having more genuine love.

So, if you are struggling about the mealtime environment you've created in the past, keep in mind you are in a much stronger position for making healthy changes than some other parents. What you perceive as a weakness or failure is actually a reflection of some healthy potential and readiness to make changes that will benefit you and your kids.

Food for Thought

1. Have you ever known someone who had to "clean their plate" at every meal? What do you think they learned from that experience?

2. Was the father at the beginning of the chapter strong or brave? Did he become more kind?

3. How does using a consistent pattern of warmth, acceptance, and delight impact your child?

4. Is it ever too late to change your parenting so you can offer your child more of your warmth, acceptance, and delight? Why or why not?

CHAPTER 11:

Learning to Have Mealtime Conversations That Support Language Development, Build Self-Regulation, and Build Connection

Have you ever had a conversation with someone in which they listened to you and did so with undivided attention? How did that feel for you? Most people tell me it feels great. It really is a gift to have someone who listens to you like that.

Did you ever have a conversation with someone that was fun, enjoyable, and relaxing? Usually that happens because there is an atmosphere of safety and trust. It is a gift to each person.

Mealtimes are a great time for you and your child to have these types of conversations. Mealtime conversations are a great opportunity for your child to receive your love, care, and connection. These are big and valuable gifts to your child.

One mom shared with me how at dinner each night she asks each child what was the best thing that happened today and what was the worst thing that happened. Each of her kids is given a turn to share about their day. She allows them to take as much time as they need. Her children have learned that if one of their brothers or sisters takes a long time to share they will still get as much time as they need to share about their day. Her kids have come to expect that this will happen each night at dinner.

Likewise, mealtimes are an important opportunity for your child to learn how to give others the opportunity to share about themselves in a mealtime conversation. It is also an opportunity for your child to learn to give someone their undivided attention.

Learning to wait to share in the conversation while someone else is speaking helps a child learn to wait. This is learning self-control. When a child waits for his turn to speak and then is able to speak and receive your full attention, that gives your child a nice pay-off for waiting. When this happens over and over, it builds trust in your child because he is learning if he waits, he will get to share and will get your undivided attention.

You are building his capability to self-regulate himself. Being able to self-regulate your feelings and yourself is an important capability to being successful in school, in relationships, and in life. A recent article in the New York Times discussed how an approach that purposefully builds preschoolers' capability to self-regulate helps them be more successful academically. [26] The article stated, *"The ability of young children to control their emotional and cognitive impulses, it turns out, is a remarkably strong indicator of both short-term and long-term success, academic and otherwise. In some studies, self-regulation skills have been shown to predict academic achievement more reliably than I.Q. tests."* I think one can make the case that self-regulation is actually a key component of a child's foundational capability for learning.

I also believe a child's capability to self-regulate can help protect them from the adverse educational impact of a key barrier to learning and joy of learning – shame. When a child is struggling with learning something new, the potential exists for the child to experience shame from not being able to do something. Dr. Donald Nathanson has shared how struggles with learning can trigger shame which then shuts down the learning process and brings up stored similar experiences of shame. [27] An essential part of learning is the learner's interest. Nathanson points out that interest is actually an emotion. We need interest in order to pay attention. Nathanson points out when a learner encounters an acute interruption in interest this triggers a physiologic mechanism - the physiology of shame or shame affect. Thus, shame is actually a biological process. Nathanson shares how the shame response can be substantially reduced by having someone on your side who you know loves you, is supporting you, and helps you address the acute interruption. Kids who have received the support and love that strengthens their self-regulation capability are better able to deal with shame than kids with weaker self-regulation capability.

By the way, if you want to learn more about how shame interferes with and prevents children learning to read, go to www.childrenofthecode.org. Shame is a huge and largely undetected barrier to kids learning to read. But more importantly, shame prevents kids from having a joy of learning.

I still remember a presentation I gave to a group of preschool teachers about how shame interferes with learning. As we discussed the signs given off by a child that indicate the child is experiencing shame, we ended up discussing the ways, both verbal and non-verbal, the teachers were using shame to control the children. They began to realize they were using certain tones of voice, certain looks, and certain actions to stop a child's behavior by causing shame in the child. I don't know what happened in their classrooms after this discussion, but I do know they left with a new awareness of themselves in regard to their use of shame.

I bring up the giving and receiving aspect of mealtime conversations because it is a reflection of how love is built in a relationship. The growth of love in a relationship is actually a 4-step process that involves genuine giving and genuine receiving. If one person doesn't offer their genuine love, that will stop the process. If one person cannot receive the other person's genuine love, that will stop the process. Basically, it plays out like this:

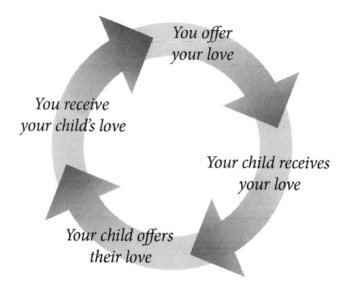

- When your child wants to share something in a mealtime conversation, he is offering something important to you. This is an act of offering his love.

- When you genuinely listen to him, you are receiving his love.

- When he is finished speaking, and you say something to show you understood it or ask a question to indicate you want to hear more from him, you are offering your love.

- When your child listens to your statement of understanding or your question and begins to share again, he has received your love and starts to offer his love again.

Another gift to you in having mealtime conversations is you then get to have a great opportunity to find out about your child's day and your child's uniqueness, including his unique perspective. You get to learn just how your child is unique. Understanding, accepting, and valuing your child's uniqueness is a great gift to give your child.

Mealtime conversations allow a child to have an experience of your genuine delight. When someone genuinely delights in us, we take that experience, store it forever, and use it as evidence we have genuine self-worth. Since the experience of genuine delight is so emotionally powerful, the power of the emotion ensures the experience is basically cemented into our brains.

Mealtime conversations also allow you to learn about a struggle your child may be having with his learning in school or in his relationship with his teacher or other students.

Mealtime conversations are also important for helping young children acquire the capability to have conversations and to learn words. Both of these support your young child acquiring the capability to read and write.

Mealtime conversations also give kids the experiential knowledge that they exist. Your talking and listening create an experience for your kids that they exist. Genuine conversations with genuine sharing and listening, regardless of whether the conversations are serious, humorous, or even silly, confirm for kids that you acknowledge and bless their existence. Additionally, these conversations convey to your kids they have value and worth.

One of the reasons you want to build a safe, nurturing, and developmentally challenging mealtime environment is because this type of mealtime environment is the most supportive environment for genuine mealtime conversations that support your child's healthy development.

Family Language Environments

We know, in a general way, that children have very different experiences in their homes, including language experiences. We also know that children's language experiences play an important role in either supporting or hindering children's ability to read.

In 1995 Betty Hart and Todd Risley released a book on their research about children's different language experiences in their families.[28] They were able to define the differences in families much more specifically. They observed three groups of families – working class families, low income families, and families of college educated parents. Three of the major differences were:

Amount of Talking

Some families were much less talkative and some were much more talkative. No surprise there. However the Hart and Risley research study was actually able to count the number of words each child in the study heard during each hour of observation in the home. They then calculated the total number of words the children likely heard by the time the child turned 4 years of age. On average, for the child whose family was not talkative, a child would hear a total of 13,000,000 words. That seems like a lot. However, on average, for the children whose parents were much more talkative, a child would hear a total of 48,000,000 words. That is a huge difference, and it is an important difference. But there was more.

Encouragements vs. Discouragements

Have you ever been around someone who compliments you, notices and tells you you're doing a good job, and says things to that encourage you? Personally, I like being around people like that.

On the other hand, have you ever been around people who focus more on telling you that you made a mistake or saying things that discourage you? If this is what they mainly do, they are unpleasant to be around. In fact, I find I have to put up a protective wall and act defensively around people like this.

I bring this up because it relates to a key difference in children's everyday lives. Hart and Risley found that in talkative families the children in the study heard about 750,000 encouragements and 120,000 discouragements. In families that were much less talkative, the children in the study heard about 120,000 encouragements and 250,000 discouragements.

Two things stand out. For every 6 encouragements heard by a child in a talkative family the child heard one discouragement. In families that were much less talkative, the child heard one encouragement for every two discouragements he received. The other thing that stands out is the children from talkative families heard over six times as many encouragements. These two differences are huge, and they are profound. These are very different environments. One is highly supportive of learning and healthy development and one is much less supportive.

Yet, when it comes to decreasing the use of discouragements and increasing the use of encouragements, our tendency to fix things might result in efforts to tell parents to talk more with their young children and to use more encouragements. We might also offer training and support on how to achieve both goals. Yet, we need to be savvy here. At the heart of any early literacy effort with parents is the quality of the parent-child relationship.

Again, this is an area where I believe Circle of Security Parenting© (COS P) can make a difference. I think the focus on building parents' basic relationship skills could help parents shift from using so many discouragements and begin to use more encouragements. A group of people in Middletown, CT are using COS P to help shift the quality of parent-child relationships as an integral part of an early literacy intervention. They plan to follow these kids through 3rd grade to see how they perform on the statewide reading test. This, in turn, speaks to the potential of making COS P part of a community-wide effort for many more kids in the community to have a secure attachment. I believe COS P gives communities, for the first time ever, an opportunity to bring a public health approach to building secure attachment.

Two of my favorite early literacy programs are "Raising a Reader" and "Let's Talk. It Makes a Difference." Both programs are superb in taking a systems approach to achieving change in parents' behavior related to support of their young children's early literacy capability. More importantly, both have built in specific strategies that consciously focus on attracting parents to voluntarily adopting early literacy promoting behaviors rather than trying to fix the parents' language-related behaviors. Both programs have developmentally savvy leaders. Having a savvy leader for any program that wants to improve an aspect of young children's healthy development is not enough. What is needed is a leader who is <u>developmentally savvy</u> and who understands and values attraction to change.

<u>Using the Opportunities to Expand the Talk</u>
Have you ever shared something with someone about your life, and they were so interested in what you shared they wanted to hear more about your experience or your thoughts about it? I love it when that happens to me. Kids love this too.

Yet, when someone has a pattern of not asking their child to share more or not giving a cue to their child that they want their child to continue sharing, the child gets a message that what they have to say isn't that important.

The third key difference that Hart and Risley found was that talkative parents kept the conversation going by asking questions and using statements that basically invited their child to say more. Much less talkative parents mostly used "business talk."

Hart and Risley found that all parents used the same amount of "business talk." Business talk is telling your child to stop something, do something, or give information. However, some parents did not keep the conversation going and did not expand the conversation beyond "business talk." Examples of business talk include "get down"; "hold out your hands"; "who gave you that?"

Todd Risley said, "When talkative parents talk more they are not talking more business. They are talking about "what ifs," and "remembers", and "the past, and all the elaborations."

Interestingly, Hart and Risley found that talkative parents didn't start conversations any more often than much less talkative parents. But, they did find that talkative parents are parents who interact a lot and keep the conversation going.

Risley says "It's that the talkative parents are taking extra turns responding to what the child just said and did, and elaborating on it, or responding to it, or caring -- <u>taking extra turns</u>."

"Business talk" is necessary, but it cannot provide other important gifts that young children need. "Business talk" does not provide a positive emotional connection. It does not provide genuine interest. It is not fun or joyful.

If you're interested in the work by Betty Hart and Todd Risley, I highly recommend the interview with Todd Risley at www.childrenofthecode.org/interviews/risley.htm.

<u>Mealtimes and Conversations</u>
I bring all of this up because mealtimes can be a great place to have these types of conversations. Additionally, when you employ the strategies we've been discussing that can be used to build and sustain safe, relaxed, and nurturing mealtime environments, that makes it easier to have these extended and enjoyable conversations.

You also want to aim for a mealtime environment that allows fun and playful interactions to occur. Keep in mind that your child wants your love, care, and connection. Your child at each meal is hungry for your love, care, and connection. They're hungry for your genuine warmth, acceptance, interest, delight, and/or experience of having you on their side.

One preschool director shared with me that she has the preschoolers hold hands as they stand by their chairs and sing the same song before they sit at the table to eat lunch. She believes it helps the preschoolers to be more connected with one another and more relaxed. She believes this helps the preschoolers be more adventurous in their eating and better able to handle a new food being offered.

One mom shared with me that when she was a child in Colombia and dinner was finished, the adults would clear the table. Then the adults would start using the table as a drum and start singing songs connected with gaining their freedom from slavery. The songs had been in the family for generations. What a wonderful gift of joy, emotional connection, and sharing of family history.

Larry Rosen, in his recent book, <u>iDisorder: Understanding our obsession with technology and overcoming its hold on us</u>, addresses the impact of children spending hours texting, on Facebook, etc.[29] One of the strategies he suggests to parents is to have regular family dinners and include a one-two minute tech break as a way of building in some structured time to allow anyone to check into their technology and then turn them off and return to participating in the mealtime. Having regular family mealtimes together gives parents an opportunity to give their kids some normal, non-technological interaction together.

Project Joy in Boston does a superb job of helping build more singing and movement in preschools. Steve Gross and his staff have developed ways of using singing and movement to help preschoolers grow in capability to self-regulate their feelings. Steve did some wonderful work with preschoolers on the Mississippi Gulf Coast to help them regain some resilience after the impact of Hurricane Katrina. I think it would be very interesting to bring the Project Joy folks into a redesign of preschool and school lunch periods so singing and movement could become part of the lunch experience.

Here are some other simple strategies you can use at mealtimes in order to use conversations to support your child's healthy development.

- Share your thinking aloud in front of your child. For example, when offering a new food you might say aloud, "Hmmm. I've never tried this food before. I'm going to put a tiny amount on my plate. Now I'm going to smell it. Now I'm going to touch it with my fork. Now I'm going to be a little adventurous and take the tiniest bite I can take. You know what, if I don't like it I'm going to politely put the bite into my paper napkin."

- Ask your child to share the best thing that happened to her today and the worst thing that happened to her today.

- Share part of a story and ask your child what she thinks will happen next.

- Share what your stomach is telling you about how hungry or full you are at the beginning of a meal. Do the same thing in the middle of the meal and towards the end. Go around the table and have each person do the same.

- When eating out, order a food no one has ever eaten and have each person share what they think the food will be like (taste, smell, texture). When it arrives provide a small amount to each person to try, if they want to try it. Have it person share what it was like and how it was different than expected.

- Share a story from your past.

- Share your silliness. That brings joy, fun, and emotional safety to a mealtime.

- Talk about events that happened with your child in the past.

- Talk about an event that will be happening in the future.

- Ask your child" "If you could have a friend over all day, who would you choose and what would you do together?"

- Use mealtimes as opportunities to discuss subjects that will expand your children's knowledge of issues related to the world outside the family or to discuss moral issues of the day.

- Use mealtime to share about an experience of having a disagreement at work with your boss or co-worker. Cynthia McFadden, a co-anchor of Nightline did this at a mealtime. Her purpose for doing so was to model and practice giving her kids "permission to talk about the things they're struggling with."[30]

Dennis Linn, Sheila Linn, and Matthew Linn are some of my favorite authors. They have written a number of books designed to help people receive more genuine love and to become aware of and remove the barriers that each of us may have to receiving love. One of their books is titled <u>Sleeping with Bread: Holding What Gives You Life</u>.[31] In the book they discuss the power of asking questions each day or even when gathered with friends. I bring this up because some of the questions parents can ask their kids at meals can be a wonderful practice to help build their child's capability to think about their day and examine their lives. I think it is necessary to examine your life in order to become aware of practices and beliefs in your life that are either contributing or are barriers to you receiving and giving love.

Some of the questions the Linns use are:

- For what moment today am I most grateful?
- For what moment today am I least grateful?

- When did I receive the most love today?
- When did I give the most love today?

- When did I receive the least love today?
- When did I give the least love today?

- What was today's high point?
- What was today's low point?

- When was I happiest today?
- When was I saddest today?

- When did I feel the most alive today?
- When did I most feel life draining out of me today?

- What was the best part of your day?
- What was the worst part of your day?

- What did you feel good about today?
- What was your biggest struggle today, or when did you feel sad, helpless, or angry?

They share in one chapter about a family that uses the last two questions. When asked about the results of having used these two questions nightly for a number of years, the father, Jim, said he thought his children learned to trust themselves and to be transparent and open with Jim and Ann, their mother. My sense from reading about Jim and Ann's family is this practice has built a very high level of positive emotional connection with their kids.

The Linn's share about another family that takes time each evening to each answer the two questions, "What was the best part of your day?" and "what was the worst part of your day?" On one occasion the oldest child shared the best part of his day was squirting his younger sister with the water hose and drenching her. His sister shared the worst part of her day was getting drenched. Upon hearing this, the father stepped in and guided both kids to reconcile with each other. Again, this is another good example of a parent using their power to build connection and to restore emotional safety. Kids need parents who use their power to restore emotional safety.

© Phyllis Meredith – www.phyllismeredith.com

The Linn's also shared about another family that would gather around the table in the evening. Each person would tear off a piece of bread and hold it as they answered two questions about their day. Once a person finished sharing about the 2 questions, they would give their piece of bread to the person next to them.

All relationships experience ruptures, such as the one just mentioned between a brother and sister. The key point is not whether or not ruptures happen, because they will, but whether the rupture will be repaired. For children, it is the repair of ruptures in their relationship with parents and other important caregivers that is so vitally important.[32] It is the repair that builds a stronger development of the child, including a more a positive sense of self and a sense of mastery. It is the repair that teaches in a powerfully experiential way that relationship ruptures can be restored **and** result in a stronger, more emotionally safe, and more trusting relationship. Quite literally, repairs are powerful in their impact. Again, one of the reasons I'm so impressed with Circle of Security Parenting© is it devotes an entire chapter to repair of ruptures in parent-child relationships. Learning how to successfully repair ruptures in a relationship is an important and vital life skill.

Food for Thought

1. The mom at the beginning of the chapter used her power to set some structure. Her structure included asking the same two questions at dinner and ensuring each child received a turn to talk. Why were these acts of structure acts of love?

2. How does the ability to self-regulate help a child thrive in life?

3. What was your response to the idea that listening to your child is an act of love?

4. Why is it important to repair ruptures in your relationship with your child?

Chapter 12:

Learning Skills that Contribute to Keeping Mealtimes Pleasant

Whenever I'm preparing to work with preschool directors, teachers, and staff, I look forward to hearing about their experiences with preschoolers during mealtimes. I learned one of the challenges some preschools encounter is having a three-year-old child who has never fed herself. The child's parent has been feeding the child. Sometimes this can be a reflection of the family's cultural values. It can also be a reflection of a parent's reluctance to help build their child capability about eating for reasons important to the parent. As you can well imagine, preschools are not set up to be directly feeding a child.

I'm always intrigued about how preschools handle these types of mealtime situations. What is great is they expect children to be able to learn to use a fork, spoon, and knife. They tell me it takes a three-year-old about two weeks to learn how to use them.

One of the reasons I like working with preschools is they are comfortable setting limits with parents. If a parent asks the preschool to feed their three-year-old, the preschool will not agree to do that. Some preschools have had parents demand to be allowed to come to lunch so the parent can feed their three-year-old. Again, the preschool set a limit with the parent and didn't allow the parent to come to school to feed their child.

The aspect of this situation I like even better is the preschool has expectations about the preschoolers. They expect that they can learn to use eating utensils. They also expect that preschoolers can learn to take turns, to share, to be polite and not rude, to listen and to converse with others. These expectations are actually acts of genuine love.

Their expectations of young children's mealtime behaviors are reasonable and developmentally appropriate. Along with having appropriate expectations, preschool teachers can also teach the children how to handle a variety of situations so the child learns the basic skills that help keep a mealtime pleasant.

One teacher shared with me about an incident in which there was one serving of an entrée left on the platter. Several kids wanted it. This could have easily deteriorated into a situation in which several kids had hurt feelings. The teacher asked the kids to raise their hand if they wanted the last piece. She then said, "We have one piece left, but several people want it. How can we handle this in a fair way?" Eventually, the kids decided the fair thing to do would be to cut the last piece into equal size pieces so each kid got some. I liked how this teacher turned this situation into a problem solving and collaborative learning opportunity that allowed the kids to develop a fair solution and a solution that helped keep the mealtime environment pleasant.

Preschools that serve lunch and snacks offer many more learning opportunities at mealtime for kids than preschools that have kids bring their own lunch and snacks. A child will be exposed to a much greater variety of foods. One of the reasons this is good is that preschoolers are much more likely to try a new food if their peers are trying and eating the food. As in the story just shared, kids will have opportunities to learn to share and problem solve. They will also learn to pour their beverage from a pitcher, learn to serve themselves from a bowl, and learn to pass the food to the person next to them.

Preschool teachers tell me they routinely have three and four year olds start preschool whose manners need some work. They teach kids how to use a polite response when they see a new food for the first time. They help kids learn not to talk when they have food in their mouths.

They can teach kids to use the strategy shared in chapter 7 of using a paper napkin in which to place a food the child tried but didn't like.

Mealtimes are great opportunities for a child to have an experience of receiving an adult's undivided attention. Asking a child about his day or about something that interests him give a great gift to your child – your interest. When an adult listens to a child share about something and gives the child their full attention, the child gets another great gift from you – your attention. When you ask a question or encourage a child to share more, you are letting the child know you have been listening, you find what the child has to say is interesting, and you want to hear more. That is building a genuine connection.

On the other hand, a child also needs to learn to wait to share if someone else is already talking. Learning to wait to share helps build an important developmental capability – the ability to self-regulate. Basically, this just means the child is learning to control herself. She might get excited and want to share something she has to say, but she has learned to wait until it is her turn.

Of course, if a child has waited to share, she needs to be given an opportunity to share within a reasonable amount of time. Finally being able to share will be their reward for waiting. When this happens over and over in a consistent pattern, this experience of waiting and then being able to share builds an internal trust in the child. She learns from experience that she can trust that she will be able to share, even if she has to wait.

I bring up the capability of self-regulation because it is an important capability in school and in life. Kids who have learned to self-regulate their feelings are less disruptive in school and are calmer. Both contribute to the child being a better learner and having genuine pleasure about learning. Kids who have learned to self-regulate are able to handle the stress of life better, which, I believe, helps them be more successful at work and in relationships.

It is also quite important that kids learn to value having meals together. In order for that to happen, the mealtime environment has to be both emotionally and physically safe. It has to be enjoyable and nurturing with some minimal expectations about acceptable and unacceptable behavior during meals. The key goal is that you want to create a mealtime environment that a child will enjoy and will experience genuine emotional connection. You want your child to look forward to sharing a meal together. Of course, you want to be sure that your child receives developmentally appropriate challenges as part of a meal, but in a way that maintains the emotional connection between both of you.

The place doing the best work to support preschools to build developmentally healthy mealtime environments is the University of Idaho's Feeding Young Children in Group Settings - www.cals. uidaho.edu/feeding. The site was developed by Laurel Branen, PhD, RD, LD, and Janice Fletcher EdD. There are a wide variety of wonderful resources available at this site. The site has tools for preschools to assess their mealtime environments and tools to help preschools create developmentally healthy mealtime environments. They've even added a number of short videos about preschool mealtimes that cover picky eaters, mealtime conversations, and other topics related to mealtimes. One of my favorites is the video titled "Picky Eater" - www.cals.uidaho.edu/feeding/fortrainers/vid_holder_mp4.asp?vid=PickyEater&vidid=31455337.

Food for Thought

1. Is it an act of love to have developmentally appropriate expectations about your child's behavior? Why or why not?

2. What was your response to the way the teacher handled the situation where several kids wanted the last serving of the entrée?

3. Why is undivided attention important? How did you feel when you received your parent's undivided attention?

CHAPTER 13:

Gifts to Parents from Building Healthy Mealtime Environments

Building healthy mealtime environments give important life-giving gifts to your child. Similarly, it gives you a number of important gifts.

What I've heard from a number of parents over the years is parenting becomes easier when they use the strategies that build healthy mealtime environments. Some parents say the strategies allow them to know exactly what their jobs are at mealtimes.

Additionally, the strategies allow a parent to know what is not their jobs at mealtimes.

Knowing clearly what your jobs are lets you know when your job is done. For example, some parents say allowing their child to have the power about how much to eat allows them to let go of something they used to think was their responsibility – needing to be in charge of how much their child ate.

Another gift is parenting becomes more emotionally satisfying because the mealtime strategies allow a parent to be more accepting of their child's normal eating behavior and reduces the unpleasant encounters that can take place at mealtimes. Pressuring or requiring a child to eat a food or all of their food makes mealtime an unpleasant experience for a child. This also makes mealtime an unpleasant experience for you, the parent.

Getting angry at a child or pulling back emotionally from a child for not eating a food or all of their food gives the same unenjoyable experience for both of you. Yet, when you stop the pressuring, stop getting angry, etc., you've used your power to make mealtime more pleasant for your child and for yourself. You are able to offer a larger and better gift to your child – your acceptance. A child who experiences their parent's acceptance and experiences a pattern of their parent's acceptance knows in his heart he is loved and knows he has an adult on his side. Those are wonderful gifts for a child. You've also increased the probability your mealtime will be more emotionally satisfying for you. That is not a small or unimportant gift. That is a wonderful gift to you.

A third gift is knowing you have helped your child learn to deal with new foods or foods they don't like. These capabilities will serve your child well when your child is visiting friends, relatives, and later, as an adult, when dining with other people. This is providing a skill that helps a child and an adult be able to have successful social relationships with other people.

A fourth gift is allowing your child to learn to like a new food at a pace that that fits your child's unique pace of learning. Basically, you provide a challenge to your child by offering the new food, by offering it up on 10-15 different occasions, by offering your support and encouragement, and by allowing your child to go at his own pace. Giving your child many opportunities to deal with this one challenge but with your love, support, and encouragement ends up providing the child with a pattern of experiences of having dealt with a challenge and having dealt with it at a pace that works best for him.

A fifth gift you get by offering a new food a number of times in a supportive and loving way is that you end up providing your child with a pattern of similar experiences. The pattern of similar experiences is what starts to make your parenting powerful. Patterns of a similar experience build internal beliefs in your child.

Letting your child accomplish something on his own at his own pace helps your child build an internal belief that he can successfully deal with a challenge. He also learns it is ok to deal with a challenge at his own unique pace. When this pattern of experience is also combined with your love and support, then it becomes powerful in its impact on your child. That is a huge and wonderful gift to your child.

A sixth gift is that you have given your child some capabilities to help create pleasant mealtimes when sharing meals with other people. This allows your child to be seen as enjoyable company and helps prepare your child for similar situations as an adult. In essence you help your child have the capability to be pleasant and enjoyable company at a meal.

A seventh gift is that you have equipped your child to create a healthy mealtime environment for your future grandchildren. When children who grow up with pleasant mealtime experiences become adults and have their own children, they want to provide the same experience of pleasant and enjoyable mealtimes to their children.

An eighth gift is knowing you have helped your child develop eating capabilities that help your child thrive in today's challenging eating environment. Helping your child build their capability to self-regulate and building a strong, positive emotional connection with your child are, I believe, actually two key steps to help prevent your child from becoming obese. These are also key strategies in addressing obesity in children, and likely, adults.

A ninth gift is knowing you have created a mealtime environment that supports your child being curious and learning to enjoy exploring new things. When you create a mealtime environment that provides safety, trust, and nurturing you help provide a secure base to your child. Research about attachment shows that kids explore more when they have a secure base to explore from. The attachment research also shows that kids need a safe haven they can return to when they encounter a big challenge. Your love, care, and connection allows your child to regain their sense of security and then resume exploring. A child who likes to explore and feels secure exploring is likely to be a better learner since, basically, learning is an important form of exploring.

I saw an interview of Thomas Friedman, a writer with the New York Times, by Tim Russert in 2006. Tom has written extensively about the new global economy. In the interview he talks about how people need two key attributes to thrive in today's economy - curiosity and passion. These two attributes are supported and strengthened in the context of a child's most important relationships. In particular, I believe kids who have the quality of relationship that builds and supports secure attachment are the ones most likely to have a genuine curiosity and passion and to have them as strong attributes. A healthy mealtime environment supports the development of a child's genuine curiosity and passion.

Friedman in a recent column also added another key attribute needed in today's economy – individual initiative.[33] This is another area where secure attachment comes into play. Kids without a secure attachment – an insecure or disorganized attachment instead – end up devoting energy to protecting themselves rather than being able to use that energy to explore and learn. Using an attachment perspective of communities, we know that low-risk communities have a substantial number of kids with an insecure or disorganized attachment, and at-risk communities likely have a large majority of kids with an insecure or disorganized attachment. Thus, I believe it is imperative for any community making a serious effort to have more children thrive in life to support more of their kids to have a secure attachment. Again, this is where Circle of Security Parenting can play such a profound role by providing a tool for communities to set and achieve a goal of many more children having a secure attachment.

A tenth gift is your child learning in his heart that you like him and he is likeable, which helps him genuinely like himself.

Yet, the most important gift of all is you have created a mealtime environment where you could give your child your love, your care, and your connection. And, more importantly, you have created a mealtime environment that supports your child being able to receive these wonderful gifts you offer. That is both powerful and life giving.

Food for Thought

1. Why is it important for your child to know that you like him?

2. Of the ten gifts listed in the chapter, which ones caught your attention? Why?

3. We want our children to not just survive but to thrive. How does curiosity and passion support this goal?

CHAPTER 14:

Fathers

© Phyllis Meredith – www.phyllismeredith.com

At the end of one of my presentations about building developmentally healthy mealtime environments, I asked the parents what they had learned and what they planned to do differently. Several mothers shared some of the changes they planned to make to support their kids liking new foods and to talk more with their kids during meals. Then one father shared how he was no longer going to make his son eat all of the food on his plate at each meal. He had gained an understanding that evening that it was normal for his son's appetite to vary from meal to meal. The father realized he didn't have to be in charge of how much his son ate. He also realized the emotional harm he had been doing to his son by requiring his son to eat all of the food on his plate at each meal.

I went home that night understanding life had just gotten better for that father's son and for the father.

At the heart of my work with mealtimes, I view my work as being about helping to create more genuine love in our world. More genuine giving of love and more receiving of genuine love.

When I drove home that night, I felt extremely rich. I had played a part in increasing genuine love with several parents. But, I felt like I had been especially fortunate to play a role in improving a father's relationship with his son. My perception was this father had made a change that resulted in two things for his son. One, his son would be receiving more love, and less control, offered to him by his father. Two, by stopping his action of making his son eat all of the food at a meal, this father had removed a barrier that could prevent his son from receiving love. These are not small changes; they are major and life-giving changes.

It isn't always easy for a father to change. But, change is easier when a father allows his heart to be touched, as in the story above, and is offered some new tools he can use with his parenting. It has been quite fascinating and very encouraging to see the positive shift in fathers' relationship with their sons and daughters after completing Circle of Security Parenting© (COS P). Fathers love the basic relationship capabilities they gain from COS P since they didn't experience some or all of these basic relationship capabilities in their own childhoods.

By the way, one of the biggest struggles in writing this book has been because it has caused me to become aware of my own emotional wounds related to my own childhood. Frankly, there have been times when I've had to lay down the writing for months and do the hard work of gaining awareness of the lies in my heart, surrendering the lies, and praying to be filled with the truth about myself.

I think mealtimes can be a great place for fathers to build emotional connection with their sons and daughters. Mealtimes are an opportunity for fathers to provide both parts of parental love – nurture and structure. It is also an opportunity for a father to take action that supports his son or daughter's healthy development. It is an opportunity for a father to help build his son or daughter's life skills and capabilities. It is an opportunity for a son or daughter to have an experience of having their father supporting them and being on their side. It is an opportunity for a son or daughter to experience having a father who is crazy about them. It is an opportunity to listen to their son or daughter and find out more about their lives, the challenges they are facing, and the successes they are having. It is a chance to find out about the character of the kids in their son or daughter's life.

Kids need their mother's healthy love, and they need their father's healthy love. Both are important, and both are equally important.

I believe a son or daughter who has a relationship with their father that provides emotional connection and provides developmentally healthy support does better in life. Life is easier for a son or daughter when you know you have a strong and positive emotional connection with your father. Life is richer when you know your father is actively supporting your success in life. Challenges in life are easier to address when you have your father on your side. It is easier for a son or daughter to seek help because their experience with their father has taught them that help is available and challenges are easier with someone on their side.

Mark Oppenheimer had an interesting article on a book by Dr. Vern Bengston - <u>Families and Faith: How Religion Is Passed Down Across Generations</u>.[34] Bengston's book reports on his findings from following over 300 families for several generations. When it came to transmission of parents' faith, what seems to make the crucial difference is the presence of an emotional connection between parents and the child. Bengston writes that such actions as "teaching the right beliefs and practices" and "keeping strictly to the law" do not matter if the children don't feel close to the parents. Bengston says emotional connection is crucial for the transmission of parents' faith. Bengston also reports that a close emotional connection with the father is even more important for the transmission of religious faith than a close emotional connection with the mother. Bengston points out "a father who is an exemplar of, a pillar of the church, but doesn't provide warmth and affirmation to his kid does not have kids who follow him in his faith."

© Phyllis Meredith – www.phyllismeredith.com

There was also an interesting article in 2005 by Richard Stein and his colleagues that discussed the impact of a father's acceptance.[35] In their study of 50 obese children, Richard and his colleagues found that "Youth who perceive an increase in father acceptance after treatment had better changes in percentage overweight over 12 months than youth with lower ratings of father acceptance." Acceptance by a father is one way a father builds emotional connection with his son or daughter.

And I believe the opposite is true. Sons and daughters who have a relationship with their father that provides emotional disconnection and provides developmentally unhealthy support do worse in life.

Life is more difficult, less satisfying, and more challenging. They grow up receiving less, and that reduces or interferes with what they are able to offer their own children later in life.

Keep in mind that when your son or daughter has their father on their side, especially as your son or daughter faces challenges in their life, you strengthen their capability and resourcefulness to succeed in life. By providing a pattern of being on your son or daughter's side, you help your son or daughter create an internal belief there is help available when they encounter a challenge. But, there is a more important internal belief you help create in your son or daughter. You help them create an internal belief that other people do want to help them with their challenge. These are huge gifts to your son or daughter.

Certainly, one of the central issues fathers grapple with is power. Men who are comfortable having and using power can be powerful influences on their children and in our society, especially, if their power is used to help build children who are capable, genuinely loving, their unique selves, and have a joy of learning. When a father is the one who has all of the power or has little or no power, that will not be supportive of their son or daughter's healthy development.

It is important for a father to have and use his power. The choice becomes, "Will I use my power to control my child or will I use my power to help my child grow?" Monica Belyea, a colleague in Connecticut, does a wonderful job of reframing fathers' use of their power at mealtimes. Some fathers are afraid that if they don't exert absolute power, then their child will become out of control. Monica points outs there is a different way to have power. She says, "You're still in control, but here is what you're in control of." Then she talks about using separate food tasks, which helps father have healthy, life-giving power.

I love fathers who are comfortable with their power. When a father uses his power to provide experiences that support his son or daughter's healthy development, he is being a genuinely powerful father. He is doing superb work to prepare his son or daughter to be successful in all aspects of life.

Fathers can also use mealtimes to provide a fun experience that brings joy to his sons and daughters. Fathers can also use mealtimes to help his sons and daughters to reflect on an experience that happened that day. Equally as loving, a father can model for his kids how to be giving, how to show interest, how to show empathy, how to help someone, and how to look for the deeper reason someone may have acted the way they did.

Circle of Security Parenting© (COS P) sets out a simple goal for parents to achieve. They ask parents to be Bigger, Stronger, Wiser, and Kind. Fathers using their power wisely to support their children's healthy development while also being kind are achieving this goal. It has been quite interesting and quite satisfying to see the shift in fathers who have completed COS P. My take is they love being able to still have power but are now able to use their power while also being kind. In essence, they realize and start to practice being able to be kind, and, yet, not have to give up their power.

There was a recent story about Kurt Warner and his wife, Brenda, and how they use family dinners at restaurants to support the healthy development of their seven children.[36] One strategy they created is the restaurant game. Their kids will scan the dining room, identify a family they would like to treat to a free dinner, and add the cost of the family's dinner to their tab. The other family never knows who paid for their meal. They probably think it certainly isn't the family over there with seven kids. Giving your child an experience of generosity and joy is superb and loving parenting.

Kurt has had a career as a quarterback in professional football and is very well paid now. But, that wasn't always true. As Kurt struggled to join professional football, he and Brenda helped provide food for their kids and themselves by getting food stamps. Today, they love helping their kids learn in their hearts about being generous to other people. They also want them to experience the joy of giving. Here are some other things that Karen Crouse, who wrote the article about Kurt and Brenda Warner, identified they do during family dinners at restaurants:

- They have everyone stack their plates for the server at the end of the meal.

- Their children have to be able to tell their mother the color of the server's eyes.

- They have everyone hold hands and pray before every meal.

- They have each person share their favorite part of the day.

Here is a father and mother who are helping their family have a fun time together. Kurt and Brenda's kids must love waiting for the moment when the family in the restaurant finds out they are receiving a free dinner and then seeing their reaction of joy, surprise, or even bewilderment. I'm sure that leads to more conversations in the Warner family about why the family receiving the free meal reacted the way they did. He and Brenda also taught their kids how to create an entertaining and fun time together.

You can also see that Kurt and Brenda are providing wonderful emotional connection with their kids along with joy, generosity, and mindfulness. I love how Kurt and Brenda have infused both nurture and structure, the two parts of parental love, into their parenting.

Summary
As a father, your number one strategy is to be present at the table with your son or daughter and make a commitment to keeping mealtime a safe place, a pleasant time, and an enjoyable experience. Do that, and you've done 80% of the work required.

Next, create a mealtime experience that builds emotional connection. Now you've reached 90% level of what you need to do.

Then, use mealtime strategies that build the eating capabilities and life skills covered in the previous chapters. That will put you at the 100% level and into the territory of powerful fathering. Your kids will be wealthy.

© Phyllis Meredith – www.phyllismeredith.com

Food for Thought

1. Why do you think a father's acceptance made a positive impact in Stein's study?

2. A father's power can be life-giving or life-damaging. How does a father use his power at mealtimes to be life-giving?

3. You may not be as wealthy as the Warner family, but what might you do at restaurants to bring joy and delight to your children?

Conclusion

More than anything, I have wanted to touch your heart and your thinking in a way that offers freedom and support to you to be more loving and to be loving in a more powerful way. Having and using your love and your power is an incredibly strong combination.

My hope is this book will help and support you to create a mealtime agenda that allows you and your children to receive more of your love and in a more powerful way so they feel more emotionally safe, feel more connected to you, and are thriving more in life. That is joy for you and joy for your children.

For too long nearly all of our organizations speaking out and setting policies about children's health and development have focused, when it comes mealtimes and children's eating, foremost and almost exclusively on nutrients, how much kids should eat, and what foods kids should and should not be eating. Part of the problem is the leadership in most of these organizations is not well-versed in attachment theory, neuroscience, and the science of attraction to change. They're not bad people, but they're clearly not developmentally savvy. Thus their leadership will continue to be limited in their impact on children's healthy development, and our country misses out on some huge opportunities for creating more genuinely loving, capable, caring, and curious citizens.

As a result, parents have not been supported and encouraged to build mealtime environments that focus on helping children thrive in life. In fact, parents have been given a toxic message about children and nutrition. Obviously, what children eat is important and no one can argue with helping children receive a nutritionally healthy diet. I happen to think what we need is a developmentally savvy shift in our approach to mealtimes, and other areas of children's development, such as play, early literacy, etc., that first seeks to create mealtime and other environments that build emotional safety, connection, and life skills and capabilities so many more kids are thriving in life.

But clearly, we need a national agenda of building and restoring secure attachment in children. We need a national agenda that focuses on building children's personal and interpersonal capacities needed to thrive in life. We need a national agenda that helps many more children achieve a joy of exploring and a joy of learning.

I hope this book helps more parents to be able to create and implement an agenda for their families that builds and restores secure attachment, builds children's personal and interpersonal capacities needed to thrive in life, and builds a joy of exploring and a joy of learning. I also hope this book helps more parents become a voice for change for creating and supporting developmentally healthy mealtime environments in their communities.

Whenever a parent decides to set and carry out an agenda of creating a developmentally savvy mealtime environment in their home, I want you to know you are doing profound and powerful work.

Much joy, peace, and blessing to you.

Recommended Reading List

Parenting

<u>Growing Up Again: Parenting ourselves, parenting our children,</u> Jean Clarke and Connie Dawson; Harper Collins.
I found this to be a kind and wise book. Parenting can bring up old hurts and expose our weaknesses. I received a lot of good ideas. I loved their concept of looking at parenting as nurture and structure – simple but quite profound. This book provides lots of good tools to support reflection and to build new insights and capabilities.

<u>Raising Self-Reliant Children in a Self-Indulgent World - Seven building blocks for developing capable young people,</u> H. Stephen Glenn and Jane Nelsen; Random House (Prima Publishing).

I love this book. They bring such a kind approach to seeing common struggles with kids as opportunities to deepen a parent's connection with their child while helping kids learn from their experiences so they are better equipped to thrive in life. The bonus is they help parents do this without shaming their child.

<u>Boundaries with Kids</u> by Henry Cloud and John Townsend; Zondervan. As someone who has struggled to set boundaries and to become more comfortable setting boundaries, this book provided excellent help with my thinking and gave me some excellent tools.

<u>Giving the Love that Heals</u>, Harville Hendrix and Helen Hunt; Simon and Schuster.
This book helped me to look at my struggles with parenting with deeper understanding, depth, and insight and led to me having more acceptance of myself and more compassion for why I had been behaving the way I had.

Relationship Building

<u>The Circle of Security Intervention: Enhancing attachment in early parent-child relationships</u> by Bert Powell, Glen Cooper, Kent Hoffman, and Bob Marvin; Guilford Press If you want to better understand how different attachment patterns are built in parent-child relationships, this is the book that explains it best. Even better, this book helps you understand the powerful and often unconscious forces at work in the development of each type of attachment pattern. The stories of their work with parents are just profound, particularly in the last section of the book. Kent, Bert, and Glen bring incredible love, deep caring, strength, wisdom, and compassion throughout the book. If a Nobel Prize is ever given for working to allow more love to be released in our world, these guys deserve it. I sincerely believe what they have developed will one day be viewed as having the same magnitude of impact as the introduction of antibiotics.

<u>Getting the Love You Want</u>, Harville Hendrix; Henry Holt and Company.
This book really helped my wife and I understand the forces at play that could have ended our marriage and helped us tap into some new ways of interacting and seeing each other that strengthened our trust and security in each other.

<u>A General Theory of Love</u>, Thomas Lewis, Fari Amini, and Richard Lannon; Random House.
This book helped me understand the power of secure attachment and gave me a deep appreciation for the power of implicit memory, particularly the way implicit memory can drive our behavior in relationships. Their writing on the triune brain is superb. I would have loved to have joined these guys when they met on Saturday mornings to work on their book.

<u>Becoming Attached: First relationships and how they shape our capacity to love</u>, Robert Karen; Oxford University Press.
This book helped me to understand why attachment theory is so important and profound. I appreciated the opportunity to learn about

the early work of John Bowlby and Mary Ainsworth. To me this book read like a good novel.

Sleeping with Bread: Holding what gives you life, Dennis Linn, Sheila Fabricant Linn, and Matthew Linn; Paulist Press.
A great book on the power of reflecting on our lives. I loved the parts where parents created the structure so their children gained the experience of reflecting on their day.

Cooking with Kids

The Gastrokid Cookbook: Feeding a Foodie Family in a Fast-Food World by Matthew Yeomans and Hugh Garvey; Wiley.
I like this book for a number of reasons. I love their ten rules that help parents remember that what is important is spending time together connecting and exploring. Their recipes help bring adventure and curiosity into cooking.

ChopChop: The Kids' Guide to Cooking Real Food with Your Family by Sally Sampson Carl Tremblay; Simon and Schuster.
I liked the tasting experiment in this book as it is very supportive of helping to develop kids' spirit of exploration and curiosity. I also like the wide variety of recipes.

The Kid's Cookbook: A great book for kids who love to cook (2002) by Abigail J. Dodge; Williams-Sonoma.
This is a book designed to be used with kids who are nine years and older.

References

1 Circle of Security International; www.circleofsecurity.net

2 Clarke, J, Dawson, C. Growing up again: parenting ourselves, parenting our children. Harper Collins; 1989.

3 Circle of Security drawing accessed March 5, 2012 at http://www.circleofsecurity.net/assets/forms_pdf/COS_chart%20childsneeds.pdf

4 Hendrix H and Hunt H. Giving the love that heals. New York: Simon and Schuster, 1998.

5 Clarke, J, Dawson, C. Growing up again: parenting ourselves, parenting our children. Harper Collins; 1989.

6 Resnick MD, Harris LJ, Blum RW. The impact of caring and connectedness on adolescent health and well-being. J Paediatr Child Health. 1993; 29 Suppl 1: S3-9.

7 Musick, M and Meier, A. Assessing causality and persistence in associations between family dinners and adolescent well-being. Journal of Marriage and Family. 2012;74:476-493.

8 Lewis T, Amini F, Lannon R. A general theory of love. New York: Random House, 2000.

9 (Accessed 4/8/08 http://committedparent.wordpress.com/2008/02/09/on-skillfully-speaking-truth-to-power/;Muriel-murielhastings@mac.com

10 Cloud H, Townsend J. Boundaries with kids. Grand Rapids (MI): Zondervan; 1998, Page 52.

[11] Glenn, H, Nelsen, J. Raising self-reliant children in a self-indulgent world - seven building blocks for developing capable young people. 1997.

[12] Birch L, McPhee L, Shoba B, Pirok E, Steinberg L. What kind of exposure reduces children's food neophobia? Appetite. 1987; 9:171-178.

[13] Carruth B, Ziegler P, Gordon A, Barr S. Prevalence of picky eaters among infants and toddlers and their caregivers' decisions about offering a new food. J Am Diet Assoc. 2004;104: S57-S64.

[14] Wardle J, Cooke L, Gibson E, Sapochnika M, Sheiham A, Lawson M. Increasing children's acceptance of vegetables; a randomized trial of parent-led exposure. Appetite. 2003; 40:155–162.

[15] McGrath J. Heartbeat: George Bush in his own words. New York: Simon and Schuster, 2001, p.324.

[16] Bartoshuk LM, Duffy VB, Lucchina LA, Prutkin J, Fast K. PROP (6-n-propylthiouracil) supertasters and the saltiness of NaCl. Ann N Y Acad Sci. 1998 Nov 30;855:793-6.

[17] Parker-Pope T. 6 Food Mistakes Parents Make. New York Times. 9/15/2008.

[18] Johnson SL. Improving preschoolers' self-regulation of energy intake. Pediatrics 2000;106;1429-1435.

[19] Heckman J. The economics of inequality: the value of early childhood education. American Educator 2011;35(1); 31-35, 47.

[20] Heckman J. Schools, skills, and synapses. Discussion paper no. 3515 2008. Institute for the Study of Labor.

21 Karen R. Becoming attached: first relationships and how they shape our capacity to love. New York: Oxford University Press, 1998.

22 Hoffman K.T., Marvin R.S., Cooper G., Powell B. (2006). Changing Toddlers' and Preschoolers' Attachment Classifications: The Circle of Security Intervention. J Consult Clin Psychol. Dec;74(6):1017-26.

23 Lewis T, Amini F, Lannon R. A general theory of love. New York: Random House, 2000.

24 Satter, E. How to Get Your Kid to Eat, But Not Too Much. Palo Alto, Bull Publishing, 1987.

25 Slaughter C and Bryant A. Hungry for love: the feeding relationship in the psychological development of young children. The Permanente Journal/ Winter 2004/ Volume 8 No. 1, p. 23-29.

26 Tough P. Can the Right Kinds of Play Teach Self-Control? New York Times Magazine, September 27, 2009.

27 Interview with Dr. Donald L. Nathanson. The Role of Affect in Learning – How Shame Exacerbates Reading Difficulties. Accessed 8/24/07 at http://www.childrenofthecode.org/interviews/nathanson.htm

28 Hart B and Risley T, Meaningful differences in the everyday experience of young american children. Baltimore: Brookes Publishing, 1995.

29 Rosen, Larry. iDisorder: Understanding our obsession with technology and overcoming its hold on us (2013). Palgrave Macmillan

30 Dominus, Susan, Table Talk: The new family dinner. New York Times Sunday Styles section, April 29, 2012.

[31] Linn D, Linn S, Linn M, Sleeping with bread: holding what gives you life. Mahwah, NJ: Paulist Press, 1995.

[32] Lewis, J: Repairing the bond in important relationships: A dynamic for personality maturation. Am J Psychiatry 2000; 157:1375-1378.

[33] Tom Friedman, It's p.q. and c.q. as much as i.q., New York Times, January 29, 2013.

[34] Mark E. Oppenheimer, Book explores ways faith is kept, or lost, over generations, New York Times, February 1, 2014

[35] Stein R, Epstein L, Raynor H, Kilanowski C, Paluch R. The influence of parenting change on pediatric weight control. Obesity Research (2005) 13, 1749-1755.

[36] Karen Crouse, Warner sets example for his family and the cardinals, New York Times, September 26, 2008.

Made in the USA
Middletown, DE
02 December 2017